D1456808

THREE MOBS

Labor, Church and Mafia

THREE MOBS

MOBS

Labor, Church and Mafia

Wilfrid Sheed

SHEED AND WARD, INC.
Subsidiary of Universal Press Syndicate
NEW YORK

Library of Congress Catalog Card Number 74-1546
ISBN: 0-8362-0586-3

FOR BOB MANNING

The one that got away

Contents

Acknowledgments

These are few but heavy. First Judy Ramsey, who researched the Labor movement as it has seldom been researched before, providing along the way far more information than I had room to use, and in a form that was ready for use (not just a sack full of papers emptied over my head). It was like working with another writer—which is not surprising since Ms. Ramsey *is* another writer, specializing up to now in fine medical reporting. Judy was also a first-rate interviewer, whose only problem was that she frequently knew more than the people she interviewed. I would also like to thank the many Labor people who cooperated with us unreservedly—some of them all the way through the drawn-out project. Since the piece was not greeted with unequivocal applause by the Movement, I shall do them the favor of not mentioning their names. You know who you are, and thank you. (Incidentally, the "anonymous spokesmen" referred to so often in the essay are anonymous for the same reason.)

Next, two editors, Barbara Epstein of the *New York Review of Books,* and Bob Manning of the *Atlantic Monthly.* A writer of short pieces has a tendency to pull over to the side and rest a lot and these two know the exact moment to haul him back on his feet. I picture Bob Manning in particular bicycling alongside with encouragement and martinis as we staggered toward the finish. Barbara Epstein was particularly understanding in allowing me to write essays under the guise of book reviews and in general to lay about me in ways that tend to make editors nervous. Although it goes against the grain, I would also like to thank them both for their suggestions on the final texts: not to implicate them in my opinions, but to acknowledge a real debt.

Next a couple of apologies. Reviews planted in essays tend to be unsatisfactory reviews. There is, specifically in the Catholics chapter, much more to be said about some of the books in question than you're going to find here. Since certain transient judgments are about to be given fresh life in book form, it should be stressed that the Messrs. Wills, Cogley, etc. were being used as illustrations, not review objects and that their books have many virtues it didn't suit my purpose to mention.

Finally: I have resisted the (passingly mild) temptation to update the pieces because I would never be done. I would, however, like to register satisfaction over the sentencing of W. A. (Tony) Boyle for complicity in the Yablonski murders. I see that the state of Pennsylvania has reinstituted the death penalty (second prize must be *two* weeks in Philadelphia) but I wouldn't wish that on Tony: just a few months in the coal mines that he did so little to improve. I also note that, in denouncing his old footsie partner Richard Nixon, George Meany has lived up to his highest comic standards.

And to all a good night.

Some Notes on Subcultures

Although these pieces were assigned separately, they were written from a single impulse: to explore some of those second or third class nations which we all belong to and which supplement our passport descriptions. In a disorganized country like this, where you can still pretty much make yourself up as you go along, these secondary allegiances do much of the work that class, family, and religion do elsewhere. America is uniquely the home of the personal question: the bad news that an Englishman reveals with his face, voice, and necktie has to be asked over here by everyone from credit companies to neighbors to ourselves. And these groups, religions, unions, etc. provide acceptable answers; they help to fill in the blank face of the free man and as such would be necessary even if they had no further content, like sporting clubs.

But our austere political constitution further ordains great gaps in the national life which have to be filled in by someone: thus no national church, no official culture, no national government in the usual sense. And again these subgroups are expected to supply these needs, in a fashion generally understood to be American. The ground rules are that such groups must be powerful enough to do the job, but no more powerful than that; distinctive but not too distinctive; in a word national, but not officially national. No society has ever allowed truly foreign bodies, or automonous power centers, to dwell in it for long.* America licenses, naturalizes, semi-officializes all its institutions, even its criminal ones, and they in turn must fight like tigers for survival and identity. That is my subject. The need of individuals to belong to something different, but not foreign; the need of the groups they belong to to remain themselves without arousing the suspicion or vengeance of society.

It will be noted that I call the Mafia "an organism within an organism, or cancer"; and the Catholic liturgical year, "a life within a life"—but is this not also a cancer? The difference is slight, and it particularly devils those subcultures which have no legitimate business except telling people how to live, i.e., religions. Traditionally, a powerful religion is either an organ of the state or an enemy; (in contrast a weak religion may be an organ of neighborhood, or no

*If big business appears to be exempt from this law, it is because business is at the very center of our society: snuggles so close to power and is so culturally neutral and colorless that it is indistinguishable from power itself. Even so, big business is careful to renegotiate its status and its image as chronically as labor does. The multi-nationals are, of course, genuinely autonomous power centers, and it will be interesting to see what we do about them: some kind of international political counter-force would seem logical—equivalent to the multi-national unionism proposed in Europe—but I wouldn't bet on it.

organ at all, merely loose skin and no one the wiser—hence America's preference for weak religions). A powerful religion outside the political system is in constant tension, forever renegotiating its position, drawing closer to the State power and recoiling from it, and taking now more, now less part in the common life. Jewish experience shows how easily subgroups are taken for cancers, however benign they may be. Society doesn't like people whispering in corners.

The church-state clause of the constitution has required some truly elephantine maneuverings from American Catholics as they shuffled between super-patriotism and narrow interest lobbying. Cardinal Spellman's jackboots belong by now to the history of farce, yet they represented this subgroup at its jauntiest. This illustrates an awkward point about subcultures—that they need something to do, besides just be themselves. Political involvement, however foolish, served to fortify the Church as a culture, in the same sense that Zionism fortifies Judaism, and makes its practice exciting to many formerly indifferent Jews: or so I surmise. Political power is something solid in the world of fact for a culture to group around—so much so that major art and religion can barely exist without it. Without a political purpose, religion becomes arbitrary, a club you may or may not go to. Thus the Church's relative retreat from politics makes Catholics less identifiable, less sure who they are, less energetic and satisfied about being Catholic at all. The right-to-lifers, at their screaming rallies, are, among other things, asserting their pleasure at being fully Catholics again. To ask people to go to church, but not to march, or to march but without banners, is a bit too much.

The Mafia gets along better just being a cancer. It makes no weakening gestures at assimilation or ingratiation. Yet to judge from Bill Bonnano's musings in *Honor Thy Father,* its leaders like to present themselves as typical American businessmen, to anyone they're free to talk to, and their identification with America's cause in Vietnam was at least as great as George Meany's or Spellman's. At the same time, their lives are ritualistically Italian. It would be disingenuous to suppose that the Mafia stays in business to preserve these matters of style; yet it is a curious accident of history that both organized crime and organized Christianity in their respective diasporas find it useful to maintain Italian *bella figura* as their official styles.

After this evil parody of a subculture, the Labor movement looks like all business, so to speak, with style a quite secondary consideration. Unlike our other two, Labor is indigenous and doesn't have to prove its American-ness even as much as the Mafia does. Still, the cancer metaphor holds as it must for all living subcultures, and with it the question of appearances. Labor must constantly renegotiate its status like the Church and even the Mafia. It must insist that it is not growing separately and that its interests are America's. Yet it cannot become an organ of the state, without disappearing altogether as an entity. This is at least as much a problem in P.R., or styling, as in substance.

Hence, when Labor appears to be at odds with government, it is always on behalf of the real America, the people. When it is all too chummy with the government, it must appear not to be. Every deal is walled around with bellicose statements. It must not be a tool of government but it must not be subversive; it must not say that what is good for G.M. (or rather AFL-CIO) is good for America, but it had better believe it. These are necessary exercises in survival. Above all, official labor cannot afford to lose its formalized, quasi-ecclesiastical style, the grainy dignity which confirms it as an American institution. (When the Church shed its style it found it had nothing on underneath. What Labor wears underneath remains well-hidden.)

The need to maintain the protection of style was confirmed for me by the response to my article on Labor, when it first appeared a short while ago in the *Atlantic Monthly*. The bitterest complaints, transcending all questions of fact, concerned my jokes— though whether because these were bad, or just because they were jokes was not clear. Likewise, I haven't received so many assaults on my "tone" since I did an exposé of funeral directors, another quasi-religious body, some years back.

It had in fact been precisely part of my aim to cut through the false solemnity that surrounds Labor and to write about it like anything else in America, whether politics or the arts. I admit that Meany and his Council sometimes affect me the way *Il Trovatore* affected the Marx Brothers, and I may have overdone it. (In fact, once or twice I find the tone a bit grating myself.) But the real trouble seemed to be that I had violated tribal taboos connected with survival by making any jokes at all.

For my sins, I was accused of being anti-Labor. Yet it will be observed that I am considerably harder on business and government—and this produced no response whatever. These securer institutions can take it, and my flippancies didn't even puncture the outer skin of flak-men. Everybody is flippant about business and government. But to be flippant about Labor is to endanger it.

Is this minority-group touchiness still justified by the facts or is it just a tactic by now? As a tactic it offers certain disadvantages. Much of the irritation with the Movement stems from the artificial tone in which it is discussed and the near-impossibility of writing friendly criticism of it. My correspondents seemed to assume like Samuel Gompers that if I wasn't an all-out friend I must be an enemy. Yet this could only have been true at a more primitive stage of development; Labor is now much too complex for such Christ-like presumptions. But since I am not about to give these porcupines a lesson in survival, I must assume they still find it useful to present Labor as a holy cause or a quasi-religion commanding gut allegiance. Although the actuality of *ad hoc* deals and pronouncements which masquerades as a movement in no wise justifies such reverence, or any spiritual response whatever, the tactical needs of the AFL-CIO are another matter. As recent events in England indicate, the position of unionism is forever precarious, no matter how much power it may seem to have; so the mystique must be kept burnished just in case.

In this context, one understands Al Shanker's trumped-up annoyance (expressed in his weekly ad in the *Times*) at my saying "there may not be a movement, but nobody wants to leave it." This, says Shanker, is a contradiction. Well, I guess that's right, Al. (Shanker obviously doesn't encounter too many jokes in his reading.)* But this contradiction precisely pinpoints the question of style. However random and fragmentary Labor may appear under the microscope, it must strive in macrocosm to look like a single movement: for only thus can it hope for the transcendent allegiance of its members, and manage to tap the religious, the *extra* in them; and only thus can it deliver politically. "Labor supports Nixon" loses all bite when you discover that there is no Labor, in this sense.

So much for style notes. If Labor really were a single movement, it would terrify us and hence endanger itself; if it didn't appear to be a movement it would fade, like the styleless American Church, into the landscape. The Mafia, our parody example, claims it does not exist, but its style is everywhere.

*Incidentally, Shanker's pseudo-outraged blast at my piece indicates, I believe, both why he is where he is and why he may not get much further (though again, far be it from me to give Shanker pointers on how to get ahead). By picturing me as a village idiot, he lost (I trust) a few of my readers, while gaining nothing; and his willful misreadings of the text made him seem either dense or malignant. An urbaner man, of the kind who becomes a national leader, would have used condescension: Sheed may be all right in his own field (whatever that is), but is lost in ours—that kind of thing. I pass this on free to Mr. Shanker for next time. Enemies shouldn't be multiplied unnecessarily, unless you're content to be a minor celebrity or insult-comic. I admire Shanker as a union leader, when he keeps out of other people's unions, and enjoy his column, but this bush-league stuff has to go if he wants to operate out of something larger than a Union hall.

THREE MOBS: LABOR, CHURCH AND MAFIA

Next a few words about my own angle of vision (a more guileless man would say qualifications). I was obliged to approach my subjects from three different ranges. The Mafia had to be deduced entirely from the texts—nobody gets much closer than that and lives anyway. It is, now that the CIA is out in the open, the last of our great mystery religions: even its members seem genuinely unsure of its existence, beyond their own particular cells. Masonry, the businessman's Mafia, may be comparable (as a Catholic I'll never know), at least in meeting its members' needs for ritual and clannishness. But I am not yet convinced that the conduct of our business or politics would be radically different if Masonry just blew away. Like college fraternities, its secrecy irritates without adding much of anything: therefore I list it, pending advice, under clubs, not subcultures.

The Labor movement was surveyed from a middle distance. I was raised with strong Labor sympathies, courtesy of my Irish-Australian relatives, but little firsthand contact. (I was amused by a correspondent who assumed from this that I knew nothing of the workman's plight: no respectable union would tolerate the level of poverty and insecurity that most free-lance writers take for granted.) Obviously my judgments would have been firmer and less like questions if I had spent my life in the Labor movement.

But those who have so spent their lives seem to have nothing new to say about it. With the old-timers you can barely tell what year they're talking about (which isn't senility but plain good sense: they borrow lustre, and excuses, from the Golden Age). With the

8

new-timers, you get more regional and contemporary specifics, but less sense of Labor as a Whole. In both cases, the spokesmen are usually so identified with their subject that they rarely see it in perspective with other subjects: Labor is at the center with America sprawled round the edges.

As with a play or movie, it is not enough to keep getting this backstage point of view of Labor. Someone has to speak for the audience. And Robert Manning at the *Atlantic* thought it worthwhile to assign a reasonably open-minded ("empty-headed" snarls my typical reader) outsider to "review" Labor in this way. Of course, nobody likes to be a play if they're used to being a coronation or other self-celebration. But in this case it is of some importance to know what the audience is thinking. And if my critics think my review was unfair, they should hear from my Union-busting pen pals who believe that Labor, single-handed, caused inflation (despite the Vietnam bloodbath) and is the only group ever to buy a politician (despite ITT and the Milk Deal).

My own assumption was that Labor was probably just human nature going about its business batting the usual .250. I no more expected automatic honor from a Labor leader than from a writer forced to choose between the *Nation* and *Penthouse*. My concern was to find the context in which nature's ration of saints and scoundrels were operating this time. And I found, to no one's surprise, enough horrible examples to satisfy the most bloodthirsty scab and enough good ones to please the smuggest supporter. This would have been true of any large organization on God's green earth. Since I was writing an article and not a set of desk encyclopedias, I had to let most of this fascinating but self-cancelling material go.

This last point might be stressed to ward off further outbursts of spleen, of which I already have a lifetime supply. The essay was not meant for a definitive history of Labor, which is easily available (and should be availed of) elsewhere. Numerous key names were omitted—Sidney Hillman, Harry Bridges, Bill Green, and on and on—because each was a tempting bypath leading into a book. I might add that not all my mail was surly: an ex-carpenter whose union pension had just been cut to nothing, a Chavez farmworker, an independent trucker, and several others thought I was on the right track.

Catholicism I approach from up close—close enough to know how partial and complacent such a view can be. I have to keep reminding myself, for instance, that although I was raised a Catholic I was spared the mind-bending effects of parochial education. For instance, nobody told me that masturbation was a mortal sin—a trivial matter you might suppose, but enough to tie many a young Catholic in knots for years. Also, I spent some time in England where I learned a different style of being Catholic: a more attractive style, because underdogs are usually more attractive. And finally, my parents were exceptionally cosmopolitan in their Catholicism, and they knew the difference between a Spanish bishop and a Dutch one, and even a Jesuit in India from a Maryknoller in Japan. Far from being a monolith, the Church came to me as a travelogue of distinct expressions from each country it was in, as unmistakably regional as French cooking or German music. My objection to the American church is that it was not regional in this sense but colonial: the cooking was Roman, the music was Roman. And the average bishop was like a native colonial officer, a *Babu,* woodenly carrying out instructions from abroad. When Rome emancipated its colonies part way (or at least so Vatican II was read), these flunkies suddenly were expected to man the American Church. It is no disgrace to them to say that they weren't up to it.

Yet having said this I must add that for all its exasperations, the American Church had its moments: whether it was Cardinal Cushing saying (to my father), "Only in Rome could a slob like me be called a prince of the church," or the incomparable Dorothy Day on pilgrimmage, it *was* different and tangy, and authentically American, and I miss it. (Not Miss Day, of course, who still flourishes, looking a lot more central than some of the bishops who once viewed her with amusement.)

A final word about subcultures. I believe that, just as all art strives to be music, so every organization strives to be a religion—especially now that official religion has lost so much weight. The AMA, the NAM, etc., all have their dogmatic and hierarchic aspects, and all command as much exclusive inner commitment as they can squeeze from their members. The obvious case against all of them is that they foster eccentric passions and loyalties outside the normal business of society, and the case for them is roughly the same. A subgroup can be anything from a crotchety pest like the AMA to a sword-swinging menace like Christianity as its wildest; yet Society itself can be worse. Nationalism in full flight is a truly wretched religion. And the bustling western spirit from vandalism to Nazism has shown that it can enlist the same dark parts of the mind that religion summarizes, and can devise crusades of lunatic ingenuity to send them on, without any help from Christianity. While I appreciate the political dangers of militant Christianity (although when Sidney Hook cites the original Crusades I have to wonder if he can't find a more recent example), and particularly its tendency to legitimize bigotries, I feel that Christianity in its current symbolic, or British-Royal-Family, role is more often the used than the user in these cases—e.g., in South Africa, where Christianity is used to justify racism, or in North Ireland, where the Catholic primate can denounce violence even as the Catholic bombs roar. Christianity's more usual sin is not that she whips up violence but that she goes along with it, out of fear or favor, or even pretends to ride it. A priest, or any subgroup leader, is a succulent recruit to a war effort—and Ian Paisleys and Billy Grahams are always near to hand. (For which reason, I would go along with the critics and suggest that priests not be taken so seriously as moral leaders; the onus on Pius XII, say, should have to be shared by the whole community. A pope should be *allowed* to be a coward, or whatever.)

But the true menace of subcultures seldom lies in their violence or their eccentricity, or even in the secrecy which Society fears so much. It lies rather in the degrees of compliance they have had to pay in order to survive. When Spellman and Meany and even possibly Joe Bonnano support the Vietnam war, they are paying too much. In order to prove that their groups are perfectly safe and socially acceptable, they are willing to hand over their whole treasury of private symbol and passion to the State: hard hats and crucifixes, the pride of workers and the fervor of Christians—everything goes to war. This, of course, is a profanity. The State scoops them up all too gladly, of course. If a priest's authority can be dressed in khaki, so much the better. His license will certainly be renewed. But his subculture is that much more a branch of the uni-state, and a valuable antibody has been purged.

A secular critic might say that these reserves of passion should not be allowed to accumulate at all for the State to draw on. If people must have associations, let them be morally neutral ones like stamp-collecting clubs, or finite ones that self-destruct when their work is done like this and that lib.* Yet when a subgroup does stubbornly maintain its independence, as with Judaism or Quakerism or with the Catholic Worker pacifists, we see what a powerful counter it can be to the State's rages. And conversely, we see how relentlessly other groups form anyway: private

---

*Women's Lib is classically poised between religion and *ad hoc* utility. A religion based entirely on one's sex is terrifying, a calling up of dark spirits and nihilistic fervors, and I wouldn't want to join one based on my own. Yet the alternative is a petering out in committee-work, a descent into rote and cant, the ossification that organizations without the Spirit are heir to. It will take genius to find a formula between the two. But perhaps this is true of all causes.

armies, street gangs, racist goon squads, without even the grace of religion to temper them. People must have this side of them catered to: without it, they are nobody. The humanist like Hook must stamp out not only religion but the religious spirit, the crazy drive for transcendence that illumines the mildest Rotarian; and he may find his hands full merely preventing a humanist religion from forming. The drive can be pruned, kept sane, occasionally domesticated; but stamping it out only makes it angry. Meanwhile, the crowds who used to gather round the Church already wander the streets looking for stranger cults, wilder religions. The more bloodless buy books called *You're Really a Terrific Person,* desperately making the most of what's left when you lose defining associations. For many of us the thin public and cultural life of the modern mega-city simply offers nothing to make up for the awful discovery that life is incomprehensibly disappointing after what one expected as a child.

I

What Ever Happened to the Labor Movement?

"Let me know if you find an American labor movement," said Bert Powers of the New York typographers' union. A quaint assignment for a freshman hazing: like being sent to look for Rousseau's General Will or the Mystical Body of Christ. The labor movement is on the one hand an act of faith, and on the other a thousand small movements rowing vigorously in their own directions.

What most people have in mind by "Labor" is the AFL-CIO Executive Council, which consists of thirty-five Buddhas (no female Buddhas) who sit calmly above the battle. They bargain not, neither do they strike. ("George Meany never led a strike in his life," is the cliché knock on the chairman.) They are Labor in the sense that an oil lobby is Oil, or the National Association of Manufacturers is Business: that is, powerful, but not the way Getty or Rockefeller is powerful. Most writing about Labor (which has a dismal sameness about it)[1] overemphasizes these

[1] A striking exception is the *Wall Street Journal* labor reporting, which I have scavenged more than once in preparing this article.

elders because they are the most tangible aspect of Labor, and its most coherent symbol. George Meany in particular is a godsend to a lazy writer, and to a celebrity culture, and many people have the impression he *is* Labor, all by himself. He isn't, of course, but when you get past George, it's like analyzing the Indian Ocean. The ocean is what it's all about, but one must begin with Meany, and all the little Meanys.

The rank and file may be younger and blacker and less predictable; collective bargaining is certainly more sophisticated, and merged industries are hard to deal with in a back room; but you still have to start with him, the old man of the tribe, the labor leader.

Where a doctor might pass for a lawyer and a lawyer might be a banker, there's no mistaking this guy. The gravelly voice, abraded in drafty meeting halls, the face of many weathers, and that style—watchful, patient, sufficiently charming for the political side of things. He tends to be built for sitting up all night, like a beer bottle, and his backside is probably as callused by now as his hands. He is past sixty-five, but has no thoughts of retiring. "What to?" says one labor leader—referring to another one.

The American labor leader is part of a vanishing species that never quite seems to vanish. For years now, there's been talk of a new breed, but when the new breed comes along, it always turns out to be past sixty-five and bottle-shaped. Visit a dynamic young leader like Albert Shanker, with teachers, not mine workers, in back of him, and the reflective indoor physiognomy of a teacher, and you'll find him halfway into the gravelly voice, the face, the style. No one has yet found a better model, and one hopes for purely aesthetic reasons they never do. How many American originals hold up so well?

In the larger unions, the leader now sits on a bureaucracy much like any other and spouts lesser men's briefings on pension plans and guidelines and other complexities. Yet his is the face that Labor shows the world—and itself—and he remains important for that. Labor-talk always comes down to leader-talk, funny and gossipy as a Dublin pub. Why does George Meany do such and such? Well, you know old George. Old George's crotchets may in fact serve as a cover for Labor's true interests. But they are also a factor in themselves. The labor movement remains uniquely personal and man to man. To rise in it you need, to be sure, toughness and guile—but the boys better like you as well. The fact that they didn't like George McGovern still complicates any reading of their political interest: although maybe not quite as much as they'd like you to think.

Anyway, let's take a slightly closer look at the old boy, half front man, half sultan. From the several labor leaders I've met and the many I've heard about, I'd say that he hits it off well with his staff, especially the priest's-housekeeper-type secretary (it's taboo to marry the girl), and takes a fatherly, or godfatherly, view of his membership. His office tends to be functional but homey, informing you that power has not made him uppity. He officially distrusts intellectuals, but his picture of them is so grotesque that a real one has nothing to fear: you won't be spotted. Besides, his son goes to Amherst. And deep down, he is too sensible and practiced in human affairs to hate anyone, unless there's a tangible advantage in it.

He also distrusts journalists, and will tell you how consistently they misrepresent Labor. This gives him an excuse to refuse interviews (I have never received such cumbersome run-arounds: George Meany's secretary could not fit me in for weeks on end, until time ran out) when delicate matters are in the air, and to deny the ones he has given afterwards. Naturally, this adds to the useful legend that the press misrepresents Labor. Yet his forte is besting people with his tongue, and he may be tempted to have a go at you. In which case his pride proves well placed. Although he is a politician with a narrow constituency, and can be a little uncertain with strangers, he is excellent company, often a barroom wit, profoundly cocky but amiable, and he controls interviews beautifully. He tells you exactly what he set out to tell you, no more, no less, quite regardless of the questions. Some of his answers even sound memorized and you'll find them again in the union newspaper. One fresh pearl to an interview is about all you can expect.

If you dig any harder you will hit hostility almost immediately. The kind of mild adversary questioning on which reporting depends reminds him like a fire bell that Labor is embattled and that you've probably been sent here to make trouble. "What do you mean by that? I don't understand the question." You wait meekly for the secretary to buzz you out.

This paranoia may vary somewhat according to

status within the movement. One young leader, who is a careerist playing a very difficult game, actually wrote the editor of *Atlantic* magazine to protest my fiendish interrogation. Naturally, I rushed to the tape, hoping he'd blurted something I'd missed. Nothing, of course: it was a milk-and-water job all the way. He had talked affably for two hours and was still talking on the way out and was probably afraid he'd been too friendly for his own good. (Incidentally, a couple of other spokesmen cancelled appointments after this, suggesting that our boy may have alerted the whole fraternity.)

Contrariwise, the majestic Paul Hall of the Seafarers' International Union takes a publish-and-be-damned attitude. A writer has to like Hall the way a fisherman likes a giant tuna: a marvelous talker, colorful, funny, indiscreet, Hall might break the writer's legs but would never hold a grudge. These are the two extremes, the anxious young hustler and the manly old warlord. But in between there is more caution than not.

The labor leader is also designed for function, which is why he survives. For instance, although his machismo is probably second nature, an educated man like Lane Kirkland (Meany's putative successor) has to watch his vowels in case he gets too many of them correct. And Gus Tyler, the friendly philosopher of the International Ladies' Garment Workers (ILGWU), says it never hurts to seem tougher than you are. "When Mike Quill, the New York transit workers' leader, would stand up at those Garden meetings and really lace into Lindsay and let the other guys have it, the members would stand there and cheer and yell. He didn't have to call a strike. And he didn't. If they didn't have a chance to ventilate, he'd get the strike and it'd go wildcat." The rank and file must never suspect the chief of selling them down river to the boss: so if he doesn't give them a strike, he had better give them a display of bristling menace. (One leader, who was caught smiling recently, playfully accused the photographer of "ruining my image.")

Thus, to please the members, it is often necessary to irritate the public. Bad public relations is built into the situation, although those grunts and snarls may not be aimed at you at all, but at the membership. Union men sometimes complain that the public doesn't understand them, but maybe it's just as well. The ones you love to hate, like Mike Quill, do not necessarily get the biggest contracts. The Auto Workers, Tyler points out, with their silky-smooth negotiators, might call fewer strikes if the members had more chance "to ventilate"—an omen, perhaps, if the bureaucrats ever take over from the roly-polies.

According to a recent poll, 59 percent of rank-and-filers consider their leadership fair to poor. Whether this is just the nature of rank-and-filers, or the fruit of real observation, is difficult to say: they don't go to meetings much, and it's hard to tell what they're thinking unless they launch a wildcat strike in a given factory, as the Auto Workers have taken to doing lately. In which case, leadership hurriedly adjusts its robes and pretends to lead.

The usual charge is that the old boys are out of

date. But as one raised in a Church where the leaders are perennially out of date, I have to wonder whether there isn't some advantage in this condition. "George Meany's last hurrah," say his supporters. And we think, Well, let him enjoy it. A marvelous character, George. Nobody minds waiting a few years for his vibrant successor. And so change never comes.

Seeming to be the last of the breed and perhaps even a little bit barmy is a trick worthy of the British House of Lords. Actually, in terms of Labor's practical interests, the current leaders are nothing like the doddering codgers they're made out to be. They have delivered quite well, politically and economically. Walter Reuther once called them "old fogies," but as we shall see, the old fogies were more than a match for Reuther. People talk about the unprecedented power of the labor movement, but then fail to connect it with the supposedly senile leadership. The leadership, senile like a fox, doesn't mind what you think. Here, for instance, is George Meany on worldly vanity. "Let the politicians have the glory," he says; "they'll feel better about us when we come ask them for something." Vintage Meany, vintage labor leader.

Things may seem fairly quiet at the top. Who will replace George Meany? Well, let's see now. A question for the third beer. The power struggle up there is almost imperceptible. But further down in the Big Muddy "it is as complicated and as tough and as sophisticated as the politics of the Borgias," says the whimsical Gus Tyler. Promising young leaders prefer to stay down there where the power is small but real.

THREE MOBS: LABOR, CHURCH AND MAFIA

"Maurice Hutcheson [once the top cheese; since, ironically, retired] has the same relationship to the carpenters' union as the Queen of England has to the British Empire. He's there. And they'll keep him there forever, and his son, and his son's son, provided that he doesn't tell the affiliates what to do."

This is worth bearing in mind when next you hear about the gerontology of labor leadership. Nobody down there is scuffling for Meany's job. A local fief can't take his treasury and his political contacts up the greasy pole with him. "He knows [his lieutenants] are dying for him to become president, because the moment he leaves this area, after two years he's lost his base," says Tyler.

Still, that's only part of it. Local leaders are fiercely parochial, and they may not know what they're missing nationally. One asks expert after expert to define the power of the Executive Council, and specifically of George Meany, and a vaguer set of answers you never heard. It boils down to a nebulous network of favors which may retire when George does. "He can call off the cops for you," if that's your problem, "he can legitimize a shaky strike," "he can fight for legislation." "He can embarrass you," says columnist Murray Kempton, which, in a business where Face is half the battle, may be the biggest gun of all.

Whatever the exact nature of Meany's power, real or totemistic, it reflects like the sun off the faces of his followers, who chorus his praises repeatedly and sometimes downright fulsomely. Even independents like the Auto Workers would not, in my hearing, say a word against him—possibly because they might want to get back into the AFL-CIO someday. Only the odd maverick voice, in horrible isolation, will say something like David Jenkins (a former legislative aide to Harry Bridges of the Longshoremen): "We recognize he is as paranoid as Joe Stalin." Or Leon Davis of Local 1199, the New York Drug and Hospital Union: "He couldn't get two votes for dogcatcher in our local."

How much of Meany's mystical power is shared by his cardinals on the Executive Council is hard to judge. One interesting clue is that, however much or little there may be, it's enough to make someone as shrewd as Albert Shanker of the New York teachers' union want it, even to the point of elbowing past his own national leader, David Selden, to get on the Executive Council. This seems at first blush like an odd ambition. Council members are unsalaried and untenured, and the only power they appear to have is the power to agree with George Meany. (Even a feisty dissident like Jerry Wurf of the Municipal Employees protests his admiration for the boss, and rations his dissents to no more than one a year.) They do have some prestige, for what that's worth, and broader interests than the local *capos*. They have quotable opinions on national elections as well as next year's contracts, on Japan as well as Dearborn. Up there, one can even believe in a labor movement.

The political clout, real or fancied, of Meany and his Council, and the direction it seems to be taking, is what worries liberals the most. (In what follows, the word "meany" will sometimes be used generically, like caesar, denoting the whole imperium. At such

times, a lower-case *m* is used for ungainly convenience.) Labor people will tell you that liberals gave up
on them long ago "because we became successful—
they only like glorious failures like Chavez," but in
my experience this is only glancingly true. To be sure,
Stalinist intellectuals, that phantom, infinitely ex-
pandable band, gave up on Labor in the forties, when
Reuther et al. became such majestic anti-Commun-
ists. But your regular cuddly liberal confined himself
to fretful tut-tuts over union abuses, and took no action at all. Of course, the kind of full-bodied support
Labor used to need it no longer gets from anyone, and
some Labor romantics, who would like to be figures in
a WPA mural forever, may resent this. But in recent
conversations with ivory tower friends, when the
question came up, "Would you cross a picket line?"
the answer was: "Just about never."

It would be truer to say, on behalf of the wishy-
washy liberals, that Labor has pulled away from
them. Liberal loyalty has tended to be stubborn to the
point of sentimentality. If you are a liblab over forty,
you will have weathered quite a few temptations to
abandon it. The day you sensed that they were
making more money than you was a rough one—but
you swallowed it: the latest raise still left them some
ways behind the chairman of ITT or Sammy Davis at
The Sands. And when the plumber refused to make a
house call—OK, you can't blame a whole movement
for that. And when the subway went on the fritz and
the teachers and the garbage . . .

Still OK. They're striking me this time and not
some fat-faced boss. But a liberal mustn't be selfish.

Besides, the rising cost of corruption and official boobery probably hits me harder and I don't even know it. (In fact, I suspect these service unions have brought the most ill will down on Labor for the smallest return. Liberals aren't *that* unselfish.) Groggy by now, but determined—Hoffa, there's one in every crowd. Segregation in the building trades? You should see the Social Register.

But in the last year or two, the old faithful have begun to wonder whether they weren't being even more gullible than tradition demands (the kids may have caught on quicker). When the New York AFL-CIO dumped their old pal Arthur Goldberg in favor of Nelson Rockefeller for Governor, one eye opened. When Meany himself declared neutral for Nixon, the last veil seemed to come off. It wasn't just the decision or nondecision, it was the unavoidable crassness of it all. McGovern had compiled a 93 percent pro-Labor voting record; Nixon made 13 percent. A fragrant fact sheet on McGovern, taking trade-off votes out of context, was circulated among Labor delegates in Miami —and later traced to the building of the busy Committee for the Re-Election of the President in Washington. Meany's own favorite excuse, that McGovern let him down on a make-or-break vote in 1965, hardly stacks up against Nixon's 13 percent. Yet so passionate was George Meany's neutrality that he later tried to punish his Colorado affiliate for endorsing McGovern, and is still trying at this writing, although his own team "won 80-0," as Moe Foner of the New York Drug and Hospital Union (1199) put it. (Constitutionally he may be entitled to do this, hinging on the sense of the word "affiliate"; but a less thorough man could always drop the matter.)

Hastily, the apologists fell back on the cloudy issue of style—it was the feminists and fags and abortionists (all of whom were rebuffed by McGovern in Miami); it was the generation gap and the elitists and God knows what all. The poor old liberals, who'd gone along with Labor so far, were rounded on as snobs and dreamers, which possibly served them right.

Meanwhile, the *Wall Street Journal* calmly published some, on the whole, less moonstruck reasons for Labor's position. The Administration had in the last year or so:

(1) Allowed Meany's pet construction unions a separate pay board, which rode looser on the wage-control guidelines than the regular one did.

(2) Relaxed pressure on these same unions to integrate. New York Plans, Philadelphia Plans, et cetera, went into deep freeze.

(3) Dropped anti-transport strike legislation that would have inconvenienced the Teamsters, and showed uncharacteristic clemency to James Hoffa. (Hoffa's parole seemed at first glance calculated to embarrass the current boss, Frank Fitzsimmons. But I have it on good authority that Fitzsimmons wanted Hoffa out of jail, where he was rapidly becoming a saint to the membership.)

(4) Assured the Seafarers that a good piece of the merchandise in the Russian wheat deal would be carried in American bottoms.

(5) Benignly witnessed the Justice Department's

clearance of Paul Hall, the Seafarers' boss, from in-
dictment for illegal campaign funding. (Since misuse
of funds is the common cold of Labor, it gives politicians their most reliable bargaining handle.)

And so on. By chance, these were the unions which
also felt the most violent antipathy to long hair and
fags. Those less blessed, like the Meat Cutters and
Machinists, felt they could live with hair down to
your fanny. (One demonologist suggests that Meany's
recent demand for food-price controls may be a nega-
tive payoff for the Meat Cutters' McGovernism. I cite
it here mainly for the rich quality of the paranoia.)
Why does Labor feel obliged to go through these
contortions to conceal its real interests—even when
these seem legitimate? The Seafarers' deal, for instance, needed no cumbersome camouflage. For years
(if boss Paul Hall speaks true) our State Department
had allowed foreign ships to carry the bulk of our
overseas trade, for good diplomatic reasons. (Hall may
exaggerate this imbalance, especially in the case of
wheat, which has traditionally traveled in U.S. bottoms. Anyway, it is the case he makes.) Now with our
wheat on the way to Commie rats, the unions could
righteously close down the docks and rediscover the
evils of Communism one more time. This gave them
new bargaining power, and they used it. ("If money
would have bought them [the longshoremen], Nixon
would have given a billion dollars a guy, from a pure
political necessity."—Hall.)
Still, Labor gropes for high-minded excuses, and
finds them. Whether it's anti-Communism or the

work ethic—anything is better than admitting you just want the money. Maybe there is enough idealism in their own membership, or their own memories, to require some minimal lip service. Or maybe there is some deeper sense in which organized labor acquires its legitimacy (not to mention occasional governmental funding) from idealism. Whatever it is, the result is too often a threadbare hypocrisy that makes Labor look worse than it is. Its gross spokesmen, already grossly profiled above, develop the heavy disingenuousness of mobsters and bishops. The ever-refreshing Paul Hall admits frankly that he doesn't give a damn about long hair or homosexuals, so long as they don't disturb the rest of the crew and keep it awake at night. And even those who use style as an excuse will admit with the next breath that unions have more serious fish to fry than that.

They will also tell you they are not paid to be idealists. As Albert Shanker puts it: "Most teachers join our union because we have a contract, we process their grievances, and we manage a welfare fund, and we get them salary increases. They didn't join because they want us to support great social legislation." Precisely. And why should we expect more, from any sector of society? Even liberals have interests, but they're too noble to admit it.

One hears this same tune in different voices. The gist: "Why expect us to be better than you? We're just like anyone else—bakers, candlestick makers." (Someday, I'm going to check out candlestick makers. There's something fishy about the way they kept coming up in these interviews.) The point is incontestable. And when they follow with a list of the social legislation Labor has supported anyway, one has to wonder why they *are* better than us, if they don't have to be.

But then why, if their real business is union business, did Peter Brennan—then head of the New York City Building and Construction Trades Council, later Secretary of Labor—declare the Vietnam War the "main issue" of the last election? What conceivable effect did the war have on the construction business in New York—unless possibly a bad one? And why did the New York teachers consider the war none of their business, while the national AFT came out against it? Idealism seems to go on and off like a tap in these matters.

Or again, there was George Meany, going straight for the Vietnam War in his Election Day wrap-up, as if it were burning a hole in the AFL agenda. Why? Well, George is a lifelong anti-Communist, like Peter. Remember the troubles he's seen when Communists tried to take over the movement. Yes, that was some time ago—but George has a long memory.

This kind of argument makes Labor sound almost as fatuous and otherworldly as the liberals they mock. Meany's anti-Communism certainly runs deep and strong. Yet in March of 1972 he backed any Democrat, except Wallace or Lindsay, against Nixon. So a short memory would be the issue here, not a long one. To be sure, McGovern's labor relations were as clumsy as most of his other relations (he even managed to leave his staunchest union supporter, Jerry Wurf of the Municipal Employees, off his labor advi-

29

sory board), but Meany's touchiness is an even weaker reed than his anti-Communism. His regal indignation was a sight to see in Miami: it was George the Character at his finest. But he played it too broad, snorting and no-commenting and refusing to leave his hotel. As if he really had nothing to say.

What did he (and his AFL-CIO colleagues) really want: renewed control of the Democratic Party? He hinted as much after the election, although the more usual line is that American Labor resists party affiliation. It weakens you too much—look at Britain, where Labor has all the force of the Church of England. An official Labor Party can sell you out at leisure because you have no place else to go. American Labor travels light ideologically and can swap beads with just about anybody—except possibly with an idealogue like McGovern.

A beachhead in the Republican Party then? Well, that would be handy too. But the question seems none too pressing to our spokesman—suggesting that one isn't phrasing it right. The relationship with either party is more *ad hoc* and fragmentary than any European model. It consists of scores of separate relationships with local politicians, most of whom happen obviously to be Democrats, but some of whom (especially if you're in the building trades) are not. It was this network of private understandings that McGovern (and the Democratic Party reforms identified with his name) threatened, and Lonesome George himself could not make enough deals to remove the threat, so long as his young followers manned the clubhouses. They, you'll remember, had no mystique of the labor movement. Their idea of a labor hero was Cesar Chavez, and their obsession with boycotting lettuce must have grated on the elders much more than their long hair. Cesar Chavez is emphatically *not* what the labor movement is all about.

So to some extent this is just more nontalk for the basic Labor article, "Is Labor returning to the Democratic fold?" which appears about twice a month in your favorite newspaper. "Strong sentimental ties" are cited among the old softies, although assorted builders and teamsters have been voting Republican for years. Well, the Democrats certainly need Labor funding, and Labor needs friendly politicians. And it's always nice to control a party. But Labor can probably live for now without it. In 1972, COPE—the AFL-CIO's Committee on Political Education, Labor's collective funding device—supported a motley collection of good old boys, and got very much the mixture it wanted, plus two presidential candidates competing furiously for future favors. So who needs a party? "We reward our friends and punish our enemies," Hall quotes Samuel Gompers. And a Republican friend is as good as a Democrat, if possibly a little harder to find. A Labor contribution looks bigger in a Democrat's hope chest, where it doesn't have to compete with an industrialist's, and the Democratic link will no doubt continue in some form. By 1974, according to one prophet, Meany will announce that the Republicans have betrayed him (Watergate is hurrying the timetable) and by 1976, God willing, he will be talking about the Democrats coming home, and he will presumably deliver as much rank and file as in

THREE MOBS: LABOR, CHURCH AND MAFIA

1972, when 71 percent of workers said that Meany's opinion had no influence whatever on their votes.

The one noteworthy development of 1972 was a more efficient marshaling of votes for local rumbles. Traditionally, unions are organized around the shop rather than the neighborhood, so they cannot deliver much of anything in the workers' home districts. But this time, by means of the new-fangled telephone and other twentieth-century devices, they were able to defeat the reformer Allard Lowenstein in Brooklyn. And if Labor could shake off its endearing parochialism, it might someday become an electoral force commensurate with its twenty million bodies. But so far, this power has followed a terribly narrow pattern of rewards and punishments: Congressman John Rooney of Brooklyn kept the Brooklyn Navy Yard open (he lost anyway), while Bella Abzug crossed a teachers' picket line (she won anyway). Forget the mighty winds from on top. Labor's politics is petty and intimate down to the smallest *quid pro quo*.

Our gross spokesman gives you a look that says, "You know all this, don't you? Or are you too dumb to bother with?" He believes as sincerely as Richard Daley that the country depends on a system of deals. If he is a building tradesman like Meany, used to trading with government *and* business, he probably finds a world without deals almost inconceivable, and a nondealing candidate like McGovern near to a half-wit. Fags and lifestyle are thus code words for "the deal is off this year." "They'll grow up" means: if we can't get rid of the kids, four years in the clubhouse may wise them up anyway. "More and more of our membership is voting Republican" means: the situation is so serious we may have to fall back on that excuse. In fact, the membership's opinion is rarely consulted on political endorsements. One leader looked blank when asked how his rank and file had voted; and when I suggested he poll them *before* endorsing someone, he said, "Hey, that's an interesting idea."

Again, none of this would seem half so sinister if anyone admitted it was going on. And there are signs that in the Nixon era of neo-realism, self-interest may come out of the closet partway—unless Watergate drives it back in, like a groundhog's shadow. According to our gross spokesman, the unions need to do all the wheeling and dealing they can just to keep up with merged industries and merged government. Their anti-Communism may be part window dressing but their interest in, say, protective legislation is dead serious. When Nissan Motor Co. Ltd. makes a car in Japan (the Datsun) exclusively for the U.S. market, and when 95 percent of our baseball gloves are made abroad, talk of excessive union power strikes our spokesman as laughable.

Viewed in this light, Meany's Vietnamese fixation may make a little more sense. Meany has frequently declared his opposition to any government that does not permit a free trade union movement. But Communism has a special place in his cosmos. He did, as his fans will tell you and tell you again, oppose the French in Algeria and he takes a sour view of Franco and the Greek colonels; but he would never make the colonels a leading U.S. election issue.

THREE MOBS: LABOR, CHURCH AND MAFIA

Essentially, Communism is a rival International, capable at best of closing off succulent markets and at worst of flooding the United States with cheap bicycles, chopsticks, and bamboo hats. Meany was infuriated by Nixon's visit to China, but again Pecksniffian hypocrisy obscured the motive. "He's afraid that people will forget the slave labor camps, et cetera," says Albert Shanker piously, but Shanker "did not know" if Meany had taken any political steps against repression in, say, Greece, outside of glaring fiercely at it.

Meany's anti-Communism is undoubtedly sincere; and, primed by his guru Jay Lovestone, it is even relatively sophisticated. (Murray Kempton maintains that, like most ex-Communists, Lovestone portrays the Communist Party as preternaturally clever, and George is duly impressed.) But the cold war has also served Labor's purposes much as it has served the government's, not only creating jobs but giving the work force a little of the urgent national importance it had in World War II. And if Nixon wants to liquidate it, he will have to be very nice to Labor; he will have to—do just about what he's done.

The AFL has generally supported an expansionist foreign policy from its earliest days under its first president, Samuel Gompers.[2] When you hear the Democratic Party described as the party of war, it may not be quite the evil Republican smear you once thought it was. Some (not all) of the Democratic Party's friends in Labor have favored a pugnacious for-

[2]Not so the CIO. It may be significant that when the two merged, the AFL man Meany prevailed over the dovish CIO man Walter Reuther.

eign policy dating from the annexation of the Philippines. This is not just from native bellicosity or a desire to unionize the world (Labor doesn't *think* about the world that much, to my experience); but wars, or at least wartime Presidents, have been good for Labor. World War I was a boom period, with meat-cutters and electrical workers and name it organizing frantically, and with government obliged for the first time to talk to Labor like a grown-up. Woodrow Wilson's War Labor Board set the style for the New Deal (depressions have their uses too), and in between there was the sour taste of Republican peace, when Labor was set back a generation. The Depression emphasized another dazzling new concept: the working man as consumer (*somebody* had to buy the goods). And in 1935, after much bloody skirmishing with management, the Wagner Act was passed, defining the right to organize, strike, and close a shop, all the prerogatives that now seem prehistoric. Then in World War II, Franklin D. Roosevelt paid through the pince-nez for Labor cooperation. And it was natural to suppose that a cold war would do more of the same—better at least than another Coolidge era.

There was a further urgency in the postwar era. Labor greeted the springtime of peace, and the lifting of a no-strike concordat, with a record number of strikes (4985, unless I've missed one), and the nation felt hobbled and testy, not enjoying its peace as much as it expected. In 1947, a Republican Congress rammed home the Taft-Hartley Act over President Truman's veto—a law which proved tame enough in execution, but which had Labor screaming murder at the time. The so-called "slave-labor law" brought Labor into politics on a full-time basis, and established the terms. Labor would not tolerate legislators who passed such bills and would help any—even Southern Bourbons from nonunionized areas—who opposed them. Everything else was decoration.

Taft-Hartley summed up the no fewer than 230 attempts to repeal the Wagner Act in the previous twelve years, which indicates that Labor is always under pressure even on its good days. It made possible state right-to-work (or anti-closed shop) laws—which a number of states adopted, though some later repealed them; it called for eighty-day injunctions and emergency strikes—not so bad: better than compulsory arbitration, at least; it forbade secondary boycotts—and this was more serious. But in other respects its ineffectiveness left the toothache about where it was for next time.

In 1959, with a lull between wars and America turned inward, legislation struck again. This time, the emphasis was on corruption. The McClellan investigations had released some pretty ripe smells, and even congressional Democrats were moved to legislate. The Landrum-Griffin Act beefed up Taft-Hartley a touch, but its main concern was with union democracy, or rather with curbing the power of the warlords within their own bailiwicks.[3] Lowercase meany was in a pickle this time, because the bill actually favored his membership over him. His solution was to de-

[3]The AFL-CIO had a 70 percent score in the 1958 elections. But they may have been *too* successful. By defeating right-to-work laws in various states, they exasperated the demand for strengthening Taft-Hartley.

nounce outside interference of *any* kind—a view that has ossified like a gargoyle's grimace, as we'll see in discussing union democracy.

A rhythm is discerned in Labor's ups and downs, a spurt of power followed by a flurry of public alarm. And this has coincided by chance with the rhythm of our wars.

The revisionists of the Left, with their mania for structures shaped like a human head, tend to feel that Labor systematically courts these misfortunes it thrives on. But Labor has an interesting pacifist streak alongside the other one. In 1940, the AFL did not conspicuously want war, and the CIO was vociferously against it. Prompted by a strong Communist element, the latter followed the twistings of Stalinism as best it could, and preached isolationism until Russia was invaded. And recently you would find doves even in war-related industries. I once witnessed a peacenik boilermaker in submarine work take a poke at an electrician on this score, and the Connecticut Labor Council almost came to massed blows before endorsing Joe Duffey, a peace candidate, for U.S. Senator in 1970.

The only sense in which Labor is institutionally prowar is the sense in which meany (and Meany) have been for so long and profitably in partnership with wartime Presidents. For the old established leadership there is a special advantage to this. A mobilized, slightly rigid wartime posture temporarily *organizes* this gypsy gold-mine country of ours and legitimizes the Labor hierarchy, making it almost a branch of government.

THREE MOBS: LABOR, CHURCH AND MAFIA

But since most of our recent wars have seemed pretty good to liberals, the nature and strength of this partnership was shrouded for a while. Vietnam blew the cover. Here was a completely hopeless war, and organized labor was defiantly supporting it—and even (laying it on with a high good humor) calling it the main order of business. Liberals who had conspired in the charade so far, voting time after time for antiwar Democrats only to find themselves deeper and deeper in mud, awoke at last, blinking like Harold Lloyd, to the jeers and catcalls of the good old Labor boys—whose further pleasantry it was to accuse the Liberals of deserting *them*.

How We Got Here—A Historical Time-out

Labor and idealism have gotten along over the years about the same as Christianity and idealism: let's call it up and down. The original craftworkers who scratched and bit to become the Noble and Holy Order of the Knights of Labor in 1869 were all the idealists you could want: they favored a system of cooperatives, worker ownership of production, and share-the-wealth. The AFL, which came along in 1886, was more down-to-earth: all it wanted, in Samuel Gompers' word, was "more." These two spirits have been seesawing ever since.

For the romantic view of Labor, you select from Column A: that is the International Workers of the World (or Wobblies) under Big Bill Haywood, who wanted to unionize *everybody* in one great brotherhood, and who swept the West like a grass fire; and martyr Joe Hill, "who never died"; and—letting out the hair shirt a bit—John L. Lewis, who formed the CIO in 1935 and struck the holy places, rubber and steel and General Motors, and won the boss of U.S. Steel round by admiring his tapestries—Lewis, a Shakespeare-quoting, head-bashing lion; and Lewis' boys, the grim-faced strikers of Flint, Michigan, who turned their hoses on the cops and strikebreakers; and so many others.

All this is very well, and meany honors it, like a cardinal washing the feet of the poor at Easter in imitation of Christ. But the outfit that Meany heads up is a little bit different. The AFL never wanted to unionize everybody. It limited itself to the crafts, with the exclusiveness which that implies, and in fact some of the union affiliates were specifically formed to keep out immigrants and, in the postbellum South, Negroes. It was also anti-socialist, getting some of this from Catholics in the building trades, like George Meany.

The pattern is already familiar. When the Wobblies came roaring out of California like so many yippies or beatniks, the AFL took the same dowager's view of it that we saw repeated in Miami in 1972. The Wobblies were romantic socialists, who didn't even believe in contracts and often took a royal rooking in consequence. The conflict shouldn't be exaggerated, but the AFL did break a couple of Wobbly strikes, on the grounds that they would lead to a two-union system that management could exploit. And eventually, in another familiar pattern, the IWW burned itself out, splitting into factions left, lefter, and leftest, and fading away completely in the superpatriotism of World War I.

The same two-unions argument was raised against the CIO in the thirties. But by now the AFL, with its sagging leadership, and its old anti-industrial bias, had shown it couldn't cope with the big companies above the craft level. The Depression had unleashed a generation of despair that demanded a force equal to it, and the force was John L. Lewis.

At first, the CIO embodied some of the romantic radicalism that liberals crave, not to mention a number of outright Communists. But the Communists, as usual, promptly proceeded to give radicalism a bad name. After opposing World War II extravagantly, pursuant to the Hitler-Stalin pact of 1939, they went roaring off in the other direction, as Stalin suddenly began demanding more and more American war matériel; they even favored incentive pay for productivity, one of management's trustiest weapons against Labor. The romantic tradition had hooked into the Kremlin and short-circuited, and there was no leftist "model" left, unless you can believe a Stalinist Wobbly.

By the late forties, a coherent radicalism was as hard to find in Labor as anywhere else in America. The closest thing to it, Walter Reuther, rose to power in the Auto Workers partly by scourging Communists —a necessary exercise at first, but later a tactical convenience, as Red-baiting became the national blood sport.

Reuther was the liberals' darling, and he certainly did wonders in humanizing UAW contracts, and by extension other contracts, but on the larger political scale he could do little more than go to international conferences and issue statements. As head of the CIO, he was "just a pile of press clippings" to Meany. Mrs. Roosevelt admired him, and so did the Europeans, but his colleagues weren't impressed. The end of ideology had arrived and it suited George Meany, who had never even been there, much better than the saintly Walter Reuther.

By the early fifties, the CIO had purged most of its Communists, leaving scorched earth and Reuther on the left. The United Electrical Workers were expelled to outer darkness and later ten others, including Harry Bridges' West Coast longshoremen. So by the time the CIO and AFL hooked up in 1955, there were no insurmountable ideological impediments, except Walter Reuther's mouth. The hierarchy was similar in substance and style to the present one, and in fact Labor is still in that era—the tail end perhaps; or perhaps not.

The breakup of Meany and Reuther was the usual strange mixture of personality and power politics. Reuther's holy arrogance was no match for Meany's earthy ironies. So when Walter began skipping Executive Council meetings, it could have been fear of personal humiliation, as Meany raked him over and the old boys chuckled. It could also have been a certainty that he couldn't get the votes. For instance, he wanted American Labor to stay in the ILO (International Labor Organization), which Meany considered Communist, even though it included AFL members (you can't be too careful). At the meeting devoted to this subject, he didn't show, and Meany, shooting sarcasms from the hip, won unanimous approval. Eventually, in 1968, Reuther pulled his Auto Workers out of the AFL-CIO (Meany had suspended him anyway), and the strongest potential dove was gone from the scene, leaving the Council looking a lot more like the old AFL than the young CIO: that is, not wanting to unionize everybody, emphasizing autonomy over solidarity, and incidentally, ready to pursue a Gompers-like foreign policy in Vietnam or anywhere else.

The AFL-CIO Executive Council meeting in Miami in February 1973 was back to business as usual, lots of Phase 3 and Burke-Hartke trade bill, and Vietnam all but forgotten. How important is Labor's overseas interest anyway? Walter Reuther's brother Victor lashed meany for his CIA connections in the sixties, but everyone who *was* anyone had CIA connections in the sixties. What about now? Everyone I asked maintained that too much fuss had been made about it, that a writer like Ronald Radosh who stirs these ashes "is blowing it out of all proportion" (a favorite phrase). Yet a quarter of the AFL-CIO budget goes into foreign matters, so let's hope the membership is getting *something* out of it.

Such discussions usually end with the man saying, "It's not CIA money. It's over the table"—which, Radosh retorts, doesn't tell you much. Only a very old-fashioned organization would still get its money from the CIA. The money now comes openly from AID, the Agency for International Development (who's looking anyway?), and can be assumed to be spent in our national interest, as cleared by Washington. But if the AFL is still active in counterinsurgency, as it was in, for instance, Guatemala, precious few people in Labor seem either to know or to care.

Most of Labor's foreign policy seems relatively open and benign these days: education programs in Africa, encouragement of strikes in Japan (the Japanese prefer to strike at night, when everyone has gone home, says Hall; a politeness that drastically limits their effectiveness and drives down the price of catchers' mitts), and perhaps some quiet, ugly Americans nosing about in South America—presumably nothing on the ITT scale. Europe gets only token attention, partly because European unions are too leftishly doctrinaire for the likes of Meany, and partly because the job is already done: after a flurry of involvement in the forties and fifties, Europe wound up as unionized as you could want. The aim now is to unionize such of the Third World as affects us, so that G.M. and Singer don't spring a lot of coolie-made Buicks and sewing machines on us. If the result is a class of millionaire auto workers on the fringe of a jungle—well, why not? Other nations' economic stability seems to worry Meany almost as little as it worries—what's the word? geneen?

To domestic Labor, all this is pretty much in the nature of a hobby, anyway: Jay Lovestone's toy train. The International Sheet Metal Workers held a conference in San Francisco last fall to discuss the possibility of international strikes—a logical move against international mergers—but you can't rouse any interest in it among Labor interviewees. Whatever its policy and its rhetoric, Labor's mood is isolationist. Meany did not have a representative at San Francisco or at the various Geneva conferences on international unionism, though this would seem like legitimate union business, as opposed to subsidized cloak-and-dagger stuff. Only Leonard Woodcock of the UAW (who happens to double as president of the Metal Workers) has done much of anything about the multinationals, and most of that is talk—arranging conferences and study groups in the best Walter Reuther tradition. A few other U.S. unions have taken a friendly interest. Steel has shown the Japanese how to cool off (literally) a closed plant, and the International Association of Machinists and two electrical workers' unions have shared know-how and goodwill. But this is a far cry from sympathy strikes and agreed-upon living standards. In action, the Europeans are way ahead of us: for example, German Ford workers refused to work overtime during a British Ford strike; but then their situation with the multinationals is more desperate. The multis will have to plunder us silly before U.S. Labor wakes from its domestic slumbers.

The local boys have enough trouble bringing a semblance of unity to their own movement. Bert Powers complains that printers in Philadelphia will do the same job for a dollar less an hour than his men get in New York. Fat chance, then, of coordinating with Japan.

The only sense in which most of the movement is a movement at all, except in the sense that even people who deny it use the term, like atheists swearing, is that unions don't interfere with each other. This principle at least has a religious force. You do not talk evil of another man's strike, however destructive or goofy. Even though a corrupt union may be hurting a whole trade (let's say by making housing too expensive and driving jobs out of a particular city), the brother unions will stand grimly by. When Frank Schonfeld exposed corruption among his own New York painters, it was no use his waving for help from the movement; it goes out of existence on such occasions. Conversely, a Cesar Chavez, however unpopular, will get no trouble from the movement either. He may be a romantic revolutionary with a bedraggled membership and hippie appeal, but when the Teamsters tried to muscle in on his union, they got a reprimand from Meany. "Vicious strikebreakers," he called them, and his Council later voted $1.6 million "or whatever it takes" to keep Chavez in business: an open declaration of war with the Teamsters, as some saw it.

You could say that Meany is the movement—if there was a movement. His support of the Hospital Union helped them to bust open Charleston and Baltimore and to weather a make-or-break strike in New York—and yet remember, it was Leon Davis of that union who said Meany couldn't get two votes for dogcatcher. Why? Because for all his earlier help, they feel that Meany sold them out with his support for Nixon's Phase 3, which removed mandatory wage and price controls except in three fields, one of which was health care. "It was politically popular to control medical costs," says Davis. "In fact, hospital workers earn

a national average of $106 a week. And only ten per-
cent are unionized anyway." So the effect on inflation
would be minimal. Was this vindictive on Meany's
part? Davis didn't think so ("although we did disagree
about the war"). Meany had to trade someone to
Nixon, and hospital workers are too weak to put up a
struggle. One is reminded slightly of Sidney Green-
street selling Elisha Cook, Jr., to Bogart in *The
Maltese Falcon* ("I love Wilbur like my own son").
Anyway, it's that kind of movement.

Which is not to say that unions do not help their
embattled brothers with funds from time to time. But
it would surely be saner to consider these as favors to
be remembered and cashed when needed. Some gifts
are indeed hard to explain cynically—for instance,
the unromantic Harry Van Arsdale, president of the
New York City Central Labor Council, sent money
cross-country to Chavez—and it would probably be
too smart-ass revisionist to dismiss sentiment altogether. There is a magnanimity built into the life
itself—there being no such thing as a self-made labor
leader—and we need not think of their favors as
chilly transactions between electric typewriters. Still,
favors real and possible are the oil of the movement,
and it is so much old labor blarney to suppose they
are not mostly self-interest.

And solidarity usually stops at the checkbook. The
Taft-Hartley ruling against secondary boycotts put a
stop to sympathy strikes, and thus weakened the
movement in its very soul. A Paul Hall will send his
boys anywhere to picket, just to keep in practice, and
observers may wonder what those "little stocky guys

from Minnesota and Wisconsin, with crew cuts and little caps" (a lawyer's description) are doing walking out with the bra manufacturers (a maritime affiliate, believe it or not). But a picket line as such has lost its symbolic power; you can hire a couple of janitors and no one will notice. What the unions cannot do is close a diversified shop. They can close a newspaper, but not the chain of theaters, paper mills, and Venezuelan bowling alleys that the paper owns, and which supports the company during the strike. However many crazy-quilt unions the mariners or Teamsters can stitch together, they cannot, legally, keep up with a merged industry by tracking it down to its various haunts. Compared with Big Business, Labor is like a Victorian cottage industry. A company that can afford an indefinite strike, or even close down the offending branch, upsets the balance of nature. And Labor will need all its money, friendly politicians, and overseas operatives to restore it. When they say, "We're no worse than the others," you should see the others.

What will not come back to help them (to the extent it was ever there) is the old brothers-in-arms solidarity of the days when the unions were still fighting for their lives. Unions tended to be ethnically solid then; so you were surrounded by your own people. Nowadays, there is a greater ethnic mix and probably just enough racism to make such brotherhood unlikely; and there is much less chance of a healing physical confrontation with management. Still, a whiff of battle remains, like the smell of Absorbine Jr. in a deserted locker room, if only in talk. Hall reminisces about heads he has busted and still expects to bust. "It still comes down to that," he says.

Maybe for Seafarers it does—though the membership is shrinking and getting a bit old for such larks.[4] But then, on another day, at the office of a very different sort of union, where we were discussing the fine points of Phase 2, a cultivated black woman burst in and announced primly, "I guess we'll have to beat some ass up there." It seemed that McGovern headquarters in Harlem had just been burned down. The host, raising his voice only slightly, said, "I'll have the cocksucker's balls for this," and more, in that wistful vein. Plans were hatched to send up a posse of their toughest members, "and beat us some ass," as the lady repeated. Next day I checked the paper to see if ass was truly beat, but neither the fire nor the vengeance was reported. "He was really worried about the fire insurance," said jolly Gus Tyler on the way out. (It wasn't Tyler's union, by the way.)

So violence is still there, like an old sacramental, though it has less and less relevance to Labor's current business. Conservatives used to cluck about the core of violence in Labor, but every government has a core of violence to it. The core is covered now in financial and political power and respectability. But the boys like to remind themselves, and you, that the core is there.

George Meany did not speak for the whole of Labor,

---

[4]Hall is very proud of his training school in Piney Point, Maryland, which turns problem boys into disciplined headthumpers, and sounds truly impressive. But he'll need an awful lot of wheat deals to rejuvenate his membership.

or anything like it, in his views on the Vietnam War and McGovern. His subtle Lovestone-ite views about Labor interests overseas actually made pretty good sense, and were quite close to those of the Best and the Brightest, but they were so artfully concealed that a good segment of Labor just thought he was nuts, which probably suits him fine. If his views had been clearer, they might have been even less popular. The boys are readier to indulge an old man's whim than a calculated desire to keep the cold war alive. Thirty-five national unions opposed Meany, whim or no, and raised $250,000 for McGovern's campaign— chicken feed compared with Humphrey's $5 million, but remember, they were reduced to legitimate fund- raising and, more seriously, could not get their hands on the AFL-CIO-controlled COPE.

Did this represent a serious split in Labor, or was it a one-shot tantrum? "There's no split that wasn't there before," said one leader. What split was that? Left and right, of course—but what kind of left and right? Sun King Meany has supported all manner of liberal legislation, from civil rights to the guaranteed income. Vic Gotbaum of the New York Municipal Employees has called for "a loyal opposition" to Meany. But Shanker says if he got one, it would come from the Right rather than the Left. The workers who defected to George Wallace may see Meany as some- thing of a liberal do-gooder. His support for a high minimum wage, for instance, has a quixotic aspect: no self-respecting union would settle for anything as puny as the legal minimum wage.

Whether you call Meany a man of the Left or the

THREE MOBS: LABOR, CHURCH AND MAFIA

Right depends on what you call the New Deal, for Meany is planted square in the middle of that. His mania is stability and maintaining the system. If poverty threatens it, throw the poor a bone. Otherwise they'll start forming *unions*. George is quite content that only 25 percent of the work force is unionized. "Why should we worry about organizing groups of people who do not appear to want to be organized? If they prefer to have others speak for them and make the decisions which affect their lives without effective participation on their part, that is their right." His defenders say he couldn't have said that; it would mean that unionism's crusading phase is through for fair; but he said it all right.

Much good time is wasted analyzing Meany's soul—to his, no doubt, great amusement. Does he really care about the poor and the blacks? The question can be left between him and his hat. Subtracting George from the situation, one can see that an electrician cannot ask $11 an hour when you can hire a scab for a buck fifty. The bottom must be raised before the top can go higher. Meany's 25 percent are the aristocrats of the work force (although some of them don't feel it), and they have to look after the peasants. Meany's liberalism needs no profounder explanation than that—though it may have one. It serves his purposes to appear complicated.

So if Meany gets opposition from the Right, look for something truly troglodytic and regressive. The Left? Only Victor Gotbaum, of those leaders interviewed, thought sustained opposition was possible. Leon Davis, a natural for it, says it's against nature.

"Alone we're nothing, together we're everything—it's the whole philosophy of Labor." In other words, there may not be a movement, but nobody wants to leave it. Even Gotbaum, a most articulate man, is hard put to it to state where the opposition would come from and how it would function. The Auto Workers, everybody's nice-guy union, are currently outside the AFL-CIO and would make a dandy spearhead; but the people I talked to there could only repeat what a great guy Meany was. As long as George is around, with his mystic powers, he acts as an anti-coagulant to opposition. When he goes, who knows? "Maybe it'll break down to various duchies," says Davis. The new Meany will have to start all over, building his own sand castle.

But this is opposition on the Executive Council, or frosty tip, of Labor. Murray Kempton says the Council reminds him of the joke about the man who makes all the big decisions, such as ending the war and devaluing the dollar, while his wife makes the little ones, such as where they live and what they eat. Well, not quite, of course. The Council controls COPE, through Meany's calculatedly hysterical mouthpiece Al Barkan, and COPE pays for the politicians. Yet there is a sense in which a rival or shadow Executive Council would be like a second Swiss Navy, solemnly announcing alternate foreign policies and wage guidelines to a bored world. The result could only weaken both bodies.

Labor's foreign policy is not the real issue, but only the outward and visible sign of two different views of

51

unionism, stemming from its two ancestors, pragma-
tism and idealism. These are summed up to some extent in the question of union democracy, and in the
spectacular case of the United Mine Workers' election.

To a liberal's eye, this election was as clear a case
of right and wrong as the Vietnam War, and a
splendid chance for unionism to vindicate itself and
put us back to sleep. The squalid murder of the Yablonski family in 1969 had alerted even the flaccid
Labor Department into torpid action, and they were
calling for a new, supervised election in the UMW.
Even leaving aside the Yablonski evidence, which
placed the killing barely a Watergate away from
Tony Boyle's throne, there were multiple fractures of
the Landrum-Griffin law of 1959, with its fair-elec-
tions provisions, and Tony Boyle was now enjoying a
swaggering unaccountability in consequence.

A ringing voice (there is only one) from the Labor
establishment in favor of Arnold Miller and the insurgents would have bought back public goodwill at
practically no cost: just the slightest concession of
sovereignty in cases where murder is involved. To be
sure, the UMW does not belong to the AFL-CIO, but
Mr. Meany has seldom been shy about such questions
of protocol: observe his recent dressing down of the
Teamsters over Chavez. But now, with the whole
image of Labor at stake, Meany was silent, which
meant neutral for Boyle.

Why? Hardly out of love for Tony. You'd have to
travel far with Virgil and Dante to hear a good word
for Boyle from anyone. "Wears silk shirts...

absenteeism . . . never went near a mine" is more like it. And finally, "To think he succeeded John L. Lewis!" Judging from Meany's own temperament, which is boisterously puritanical in the Irish style, Boyle would not have been much missed there either. Yet, as in the case of Nixon, Meany's neutrality for Boyle was so fierce that no one on his Executive Council raised the minimal peep. Wurf, the maverick, is reported to have said, "I can't oppose Meany on everything" (the McGovern campaign had used up his allotment); I. W. Abel, the Steelworkers' boss, and once a reformer's darling, even apologized personally to Boyle because one of his own assistants had split to work for the insurgents. Liberal friends of Labor I spoke to found the attitude of the Council almost unbelievable. Even the journalist, teacher, and former official of the International Confederation of Free Trade Unions, ultra neo-realist Arnold Beichman, expressed shock—which shows how little the Council is understood, even by its admirers.

Were they *trying* to alienate liberal opinion? Let's say the question is not uppermost in their minds, one way or the other. What they are concerned about is liberal meddling. Chief "meddler" was Joe Rauh, moving force in the Americans for Democratic Action and lawyer for the victorious UMW insurgents, who looks uncannily like Arthur Goldberg. The Mine Workers' journal captured this concern in graffiti form for Boyle's campaign commercials. Here's a typical whiff: "Clarice Feldman, Joe Rauh's chubby dragon lady, who lives on rich-man foundation money . . . so she can devote herself to attacking the UMWA, thinks [the Miller ticket] is going to win the UMWA election because 'the kids are doing such a good job.' What kids is she talking about? Why, the college kids and hippy types who have gathered round Joe Rauh, the No. 1 OUTSIDER [their caps], to seize control of your Union so that Rauh can tell the coal miners what's good for them." And so on, not all of it so mild and urbane as this.

The word OUTSIDERS went screaming through their flack bi-week after bi-week in the largest type on the eyechart. After a passing mild defense of Boyle ("He's only been indicted once"), they would swing into their real pitch, which was: those OUTSIDERS led by Joe Rauh and his Rauh-dies, kids and pink fat cats, bringing legal aid and funding to the challengers.

They might put it less coarsely on the Executive Council, but the sentiment would be about the same. (Rauh: "If I understand that meeting, I really got it.") Joe Rauh carries the tattered idealist flag, which still requires an automatic salute, but he was carrying it from outside, which is out of the question; he was interfering in Union Business, of whatever quality, and the sacred principle of noninterference was being threatened. Suddenly the movement was there, in all its majestic inertia. Powerless to do anything much about union malfeasance or corruption, it still rises like a ghostly policeman to prevent anyone else from doing anything either.

Rauh is a hardy soul sufficiently inured to kicks in the head, and he affably admits he had some outside money—pray, where was he going to get any inside money? Boyle had all of that tied up in a silk sock.

But Rauh was bringing in something much worse than money: he was bringing in the law. And this Labor is bound to resist, atavistically, with its survival instincts up and roaring.

Worse still, he was bringing in a new law that hadn't really been tested yet and was still malleable. Labor had managed effectively to dilute Taft-Hartley by opposing its execution in every possible instance. This was their first major crack at the machinery of Landrum-Griffin, their chance to show it its place; and though this might not be the battlefield of their choosing, it was the one they had. If Landrum-Griffin won here, it would be back tomorrow, and the next day, and meany's crown would hang from a holly bush.

The Labor Department did its level bureaucratic best to make meany look justified. It moved in with both feet to supervise the miners' election and was soon parked officiously in the UMW headquarters supervising the hell out of it. "Do you want that to happen to your union?" (a cloud for the Jerry Wurfs to escape under). But Rauh claims: "I told a lot of them when this thing started that if they didn't clean up the Mine Workers I was going to make a lot of laws that they wouldn't like . . . at any stage that the labor movement had indicated that they would support us we could have cleaned up on Tony Boyle without making all this law." Labor movement? Anybody see a labor movement?

Rauh claims that Meany had a good two and a half years to help straighten out the Mine Workers and that his rigid noninterference led to the law—that is, the application of Landrum-Griffin—he now detests. Fair or not, this raises the basic question: who will regulate the unions if they won't regulate themselves? Is any institution so innately good that it can survive without inside or outside monitors? Catholics will recognize the question: for years the Church would neither accept criticism nor generate its own. And great was the dry rot therein when the windows were finally opened.

The Mine Workers episode took Labor a step in the direction of government regulation, but it's a funny kind of step when the government turns out to be Peter Brennan; a union insurgent appealing for a fair election this year might feel like an escaped convict finding the warden grinning at the end of the tunnel. All you can say is that the Landrum-Griffin machinery has been observed to work and precedents have been established. The old guard will now have to concentrate that much harder on keeping the machinery out of the wrong hands. In this sense, Brennan is probably no accident. Long before the election, rumor had it that part of Meany's terms for supporting Nixon was a say in the choice of the next Secretary of Labor. No doubt the hope is that this will harden instantly into a precedent and that the job will become meany's baby in perpetuity. But do not judge these things too quickly. Early rumor also has it that Brennan was not Meany's first choice (he didn't want a union man, only a fellow traveler); and late rumor has it that Brennan will be out before his first year is up.

Friends of union democracy don't much relish

calling in the law either. Herman Benson, the pep-
pery editor of *Union Democracy Review,* believes ardently in a self-reliant movement as it was dreamed
of in the thirties, cleaning its own house as it goes.
Meeting Benson in his rumpled suit, hat, shoes, it's
impossible to feel he is less a pure union man than
Meany. But some houses just won't clean themselves,
says Benson. A reformer in a building trades union,
for instance, might simply find himself laid off work,
by joint agreement of labor and management. For
such cases, Benson would favor a union democracy
apparatus, similar to the Civil Liberties Union, which
could provide moral support and, if absolutely necessary, legal aid to the complainant.

Benson is the most optimistic man this side of author and former Socialist Party chairman Michael
Harrington, and his faith in unions makes you want
to believe too. But there are so far pitifully few suc-
cesses to point to. Frank Schonfeld of the painters'
union, who fought for the autonomy of his own local,
was cut off at the knees by a trial board from the International Brotherhood of Painters, which forbade
him to run for office for five years. He's appealing the
case in court and so far it's cost him $12,000. The only
cause for encouragement remains Arnold Miller of
the Mine Workers, who did win, though at a cost of
millions and three Yablonski lives. But Miller talked
immediately of applying for membership in the AFL-
CIO. And if he gets it, nobody had better insurge
against *him.* (Meany might kick him out himself, but
there'll be no cops in the lobby.) Just to show who was
who, Meany refused to be photographed with Miller

even after he'd won, though he consented to a private lunch. "He wants something," Miller was heard to say.

Benson's dream calls for a succession of insurgent heroes, as well as a sympathetic Labor Department, two long shots in the same race. Joe Rauh hopes to get permanent foundation support for legal appeals, and maybe lead a sort of Rauh's Raiders on union malpractice that meany will just have to get used to. But his crusade can only skirmish the borders at the moment. The new reading of Landrum-Griffin merely allows that a complainant may be physically present when the Labor Department takes his case to court; it does not guarantee that his case will get there, that it will be acted on, or that he will live happily ever after. The obstacles are endless. If his challenge concerns an election, he must wait until the election is over, even if fraud is going on under his nose; which means that before the case is aired, the defendant will most likely be in full control of the union, and of the union newspaper—and of meany's implicit patronage. His sins will be washed clean, even as Tony Boyle's. He will be part of the labor movement, and the plaintiff will be a union buster.

The complainant must also gird himself for the law's delays. One Angel Roman of the Amalgamated Machine, Instrument and Metal Local 485 N.Y.C., who is applying for reinstatement as business agent (an official of a local union whose duties include adjustment of grievances and enforcement of agreements) has been waiting two years to be heard—a long time in the life of a working man. Meanwhile, a union can reach into its pocket for any number of appeals. A Joe Rauh might match them, but he'd have to do it again and again. It speaks well of the toughness of American workers that Rauh and Benson both anticipate their cooperation in these marathons.

Surprisingly, they may be right, in cases where it's even possible. Jim Morrissey of the National Maritime Union, who had his head stove in by goons after opposing the ineffable Joe Curran some years back, has made a courageous comeback inspired by Miller and the Mine Workers. Boss Curran recently retired claiming a pension that would startle a Woolworth heir, and Morrissey is opposing his picked slate of successors. At this writing, Morrissey is trying to avoid the tiresome requirement of losing the election before he can be heard. He is appealing to the courts for the same fair-election guarantees that the Mine Workers got. And if he gets them, it will mean another big step forward for Landrum-Griffin, and the pro-democrats will be beside themselves.

It doesn't look likely, though. (Soon you'll know for sure.) The Labor Department still says it can't investigate before an election. The National Maritime Union (NMU) has folded its paper, *The Pilot,* rather than give equal space to Morrissey. And if the latter loses, he will have to go through the grotesque motions of appealing the election to the winners, before throwing himself on the mercies of—Peter Brennan.

So that's how it stands with outside regulation right now. And even these very small advances have depended on favorable circumstances. The NMU is a small union where a small challenge can make a big splash. A similar convulsion in, say, the Steelworkers would be something to shout about. (Rauh thinks it just might happen.) But national leaderships are generally harder for an insurgent to get at.

Moreover, the miners and mariners had a common piece of good fortune: they both made the headlines. Joe Curran's spectacular resignation, dripping gold from every pocket as he kissed his poorish union goodbye, caught the public's sleepy attention as the Yablonski murders had. Morrissey could lose the union newspaper, but the members could still read about him in the New York *Daily News*. (The Curranites could trundle out their trusty paranoia about outsiders as much as they liked—that pension of Curran's, $55,000 a year for life, had to make a poor mariner's eyes bulge, wherever he read about it.)

But does it always take a sexy scandal to bring public action? Unfortunately, most corruption is pretty dull, a matter of bookkeeping, and the public can only take so much of it for entertainment. Reform by headline is piecemeal, but so far it's all we've got.

"Don't worry," says the gross spokesman, "government interference would be worse. Can you imagine what political use Nixon would make of it? Besides, the market keeps us in line. We can't afford to be that corrupt; it'd put us out of business." And in some lines of work that's true.

But don't bring it up to someone who wants to put up middle-income housing in New York or have his lamb chops carried by truck.

But if all goes well, and you get democracy all over,

what have you got? According to even such a practicing democrat as Gotbaum, you may get racism: "For instance, Walter Reuther with an excellent record in terms of blacks couldn't get a black on the Executive Council, because democratically they couldn't be elected on the board." On the same principle, you may get sexism. Even in a union like the ILGWU (Ladies' Garment Workers), which is both democratic and packed with women, you find precious few women officials, though their training institute has some comers. Workers can be as reactionary as anyone else, even as their own leaders, and the fact that the United Auto Workers are theoretically the most enlightened of unions did not keep the members from voting against busing or for Wallace as the mood took them.

In fact, these arguments are only pertinent to a Civics I view of democracy as Mr. Clean, the wonder detergent. Democratic unions are probably a little better than the others on sex and race, but not enough to crow about. Gotbaum says, "Even a democratic mechanism may not militate in favor of bringing women and blacks up ... in terms of women we're better than the rest, but we're bad, because the rest is so very, very bad." Racism is finally determined by the number of blacks the job calls for; where they're needed, they're welcome. On a narrow scaffolding, they're not. Sexism is determined by the rate of seepage of middle-class ideas. The first Women's Libbers got a raucous comeuppance from the female Municipal Employees because they talked a life-style out of Mars. There are signs they know better already, in terms of particular situations, if not in grand strategy. Meanwhile, all that democracy guarantees anyone is a fuller hall (sometimes) and members who like to talk, and possibly a bright union newspaper that somebody may read.

In any case, the first point of democracy is not character-building but responsive government, and here a more realistic case against union democracy arises. The business of unions is bargaining, which can be as delicate as brain surgery. A responsive membership craning its necks and shouting advice can play hell with the operation.

For instance, Arnold Beichman, a very plausible anti-democrat, maintains that New York City may be down to its present three newspapers because the members of Bert Powers' typographers' union wanted more blood than the stone had to offer that year. Powers had done everything he could, alienating the whole reading public, to the saturnine pleasure of his members (to this day, he finds himself hissed in the street), but when he took back his final hard-won agreement with the publishers, the members howled for more. And it was too much.

That is certainly the worst that can happen. Powers had enemies to the left in his own union, ready to outbid his wildest dreams. Meanwhile, he had patiently to explain the economics of each new offer to his members—and they never did get it straight, even in terms of their own interests, let alone the public's. How, a Beichman might say, can you possibly expect such people to cope with wage-price guidelines, acceptable inflation rates, and Japanese competition?

You can't, of course, though you try with worker education programs and articles in that yellowing scrap of newspaper that sits in unread piles in the front office. Even in the Mine Workers' election, with the volume up high and half the union paper given over by law to Arnold Miller's insurgents, 18 percent of the members hadn't heard of Miller on election eve (it seems, luckily, they couldn't find the polling place either).

From the viewpoint of public interest, an unsophisticated membership could be a menace. In a normal round of strikes, there is an accustomed rhythm which everyone is used to. One union sets the pace— say the Auto Workers on the national scene, or the garbage men in New York City—for the others to measure themselves by. Then the others fall in behind, snapping and snarling, but about the usual distance from the one in front.

Now just one desperate demagogue with a kamikaze union at his back can destroy this whole chain and drive the economy crazy. The same goes for an inept bargainer on management's side. When John DeLury of the New York City sanitation workers held up young Mayor Lindsay for ransom, the cry went up —"You pay that to a garbage man? I risk my life fightin' fires" or whatever. And neither John Lindsay nor the city ever recovered. Were the unions grateful? No, they were embarrassed. They despised Lindsay for giving in to them and dislocating the order of nature.

So much for the case against union democracy. Actually, neither the desperate demagogue nor the wild-eyed membership is ever likely to materialize above the local level, democracy or no. In the final crunch, a democrat like Leonard Woodcock bargains like a Teamster; conversely, the sloppiest bargainer around, according to master negotiator Ted Kheel, represents an autocratic union. He just "signs and runs." As to flashing gold coins at the members in return for votes: top leadership turnover remains just about as sluggish in democratic unions as it is in the others—or in the People's Democracies. And for the same reasons. The boss controls the newspaper and assorted promo material, which is likely to feature pictures of himself peering knowingly into a mine face or welding machine, like a bishop at a confirmation. (In the Steelworkers, I'm told, a man could go mad staring at I. W. Abel. It's worse than *Muhammad Speaks.*) The boss's travels and latest thoughts are dutifully recorded. He is the only candidate most locals will ever see in person. A rival would need a small private fortune to counter these advantages.

And, according to anti-democrats, most members are not that interested in union politics anyway. It's not that they're stupid, it's just that they have other lives to lead, and their interest is sporadic and of a kibitzing nature. "Like a child in a family," to quote the President on the average American. Nixon's flirtation with Meany was made in heaven.

So the issue of union democracy may seem at first glance like an internal matter, rightly settled internally, as meany insists. But there remain a couple of powerful rebuttals to this as there are to even the most benign fascisms.

One is that truly gross corruption on the Hoffa-esque scale is less likely in a democratic union, and this is a matter of record. Even a somewhat empty display of accountability to the voters seems to prevent such Caligula-like activities. Landrum-Griffin is easier to invoke in an open-mouth shop. A czarist outfit like the Teamsters may have some pretty cocky locals who will tell the Big Man to get lost, but in a pinch he can always take control by putting them in trusteeship, which can't happen in democratic unions, and run them out of his own hat. (Incidentally, this is what Meany tried to do to his Colorado affiliate when it endorsed McGovern.) Also the Teamsters' Fitzsimmons, and previously Hoffa, is entitled by union constitution to lay paws on international funds without explanation. (Conversely, when the democratic Auto Workers sent some cash to Arnold Miller, they were investigated by the FBI for misuse of funds.) All this goes into the price of trucking, and of everything that goes into a truck.

Nobody could be as corrupt as the Teamsters are believed to be—and they're presumably not so themselves, although newspaper accounts have suggested that they may have had a finger in the Watergate, and they don't even have time to deny all the reported Mafia links—but nobody knows for sure because of their murky constitutional procedure. And this cruddy reputation hurts the whole labor movement and brings on the clamor for outside interference. If meany proceeds to dilute Landrum-Griffin as he did Taft-Hartley, he will have to face the whole rumpus again when the tide turns—and maybe a rumpus with teeth in it, if that's your kind of metaphor.

Secondly, a boss like Tony Boyle not only lines his own pockets, he also signs bad contracts for his men. Arnold Miller accused him of ignoring work-safety rules, pensions, and just about everything else. Boyle, as ever, is an extreme example: but work safety is something of a symbol. Remote, autocratic unions, such as the building trades', are often careless about it (hence the tardy recognition of asbestos poisoning cases in construction). A lazy negotiator may sacrifice it for the sake of a gleaming pay packet, which actually costs the company less. A responsive membership might look at its contracts more closely.

A less conclusive reason would be that democracy is somehow what unions are all about, in the public mind at least—if not historically as an ideal. If you want to go on singing about Joe Hill and the Wobblies, you'd better believe that Arnold Miller is a better man than Tony Boyle, for all the bullyboy swagger of Boyle's public relations. Meany would like to have it both ways: the defiant comradely tradition and the simplicities of one-man rule. I don't know if meany still sings Joe Hill—maybe he does, like an old hymn in another language; but anyway he should, because old Joe has bought him credit, the way saints buy credit for the Vatican. And meany had better make pretty good friends with Mammon if he plans to give up that credit.

The Blue-Collar Worker as Sociologists' Plaything

Studies of the blue-collar worker tend inevitably to

be either too vague or too narrow. A mine worker may live in a different time capsule from a skilled auto worker, with a world view geared to the 1900s; so there's not much point in talking about increased blue-collar restlessness and alienation, as government reports tend so gravely to do. Conversely, polling a hundred paper workers in Vermont gives you nothing but poetry, if that; it doesn't tell you about paper workers in Oregon, let alone garment workers in New York. The wild variety of work in America is flattened out by the very word "blue-collar." Another bottomless well has been opened up for the social sciences, without much in it for the rest of us.

The recent discovery of job discontent is especially unstartling. In a craft union, it may be significant—maybe the old boys *did* like painting in the corners as much as they now think they did, and maybe their sons *are* even lazier than old men have always thought young men to be. But on the assembly line, discontent is a constant, and the only change has been in the freedom to express it. Few sane men would work on the line if they didn't have to.[5] So if absenteeism and alcoholism are on the increase, as reported, it should be recalled that these practices once got a man fired on the spot. Unions have steadily expanded their say in hiring and firing matters; and

[5]"You would think that twenty to twenty-five years ago, workers in the Ford and G.M. plants got finished in a day and thought, Well, I've done a day's work. That's great. Bullshit. They always hated the line."—Brendan Sexton, former Education Director, UAW.

what with review boards and delays, an employer may feel that firing a drunk is more trouble than it's worth. (If this keeps up, line workers may begin to rival writers in these particular vices.)

The issue of hiring and firing happens to be a major cause of resentment against organized labor. A restaurant owner I know pays way above union rates for the privilege of controlling his staff, and there must be many like him. Yet union spokesmen seem reluctant to discuss it at all.

"No one likes to negotiate for the incompetent worker," says B. J. Widick, professor of industrial relations in the Graduate School of Business at Columbia University. And as unionism approaches such skilled professions as teaching, the question becomes ever more delicate. Albert Shanker takes the view that college presidents, high school principals, and so on are no more interested in quality hiring than unions are; but this presupposes a heap of vindictiveness and favoritism in management. Anyway, the real problem is quality firing (one department chairman I know is worn to a shadow trying to replace a knuckle-headed language teacher). And here Shanker acknowledges difficulties, although not half as many as his critics. In general, is it possible to say that some workers have gone from too little protection to too much? Presumably if the boss can no longer discipline his employees, there's no one to do it but the union. But its hard to find cases where this happens. Again, the noninterfering vacuum obtains: nobody else can and we won't. So the goof-off worker is blamed on the culture, the long-haired life-style, instead.

Can one go even further and say that Labor is slyly contributing to the permissiveness its leaders denounce? It would be surprising if not. That is Labor's natural object: to shorten working hours, lengthen vacations, and hasten retirement, and to bargain for all the permissiveness it can get. Cant about the work ethic notwithstanding, unionism has done as much as anything to upend those famous Old Values and loosen the Iron Grip of Authority. The pathos is that the old boys don't like what they've wrought and hence groan about a decline in the national life, as if they had nothing to do with the national life themselves.

One of the things that make American collective bargaining an art rather than a routine is that the bosses are bargaining precisely for the kind of welfare that governments commonly provide in other Western countries. Labor is a welfare state, for its own members at least, and the complaints about the young are about what you'd expect in a welfare state.

If workers cannot be bullied into proper behavior, the logical thing to do would be to make the work itself more appealing. But meany's puritanical soul resists this kind of mushy Deweyism. "If you want to enrich the job, enrich the paycheck," says William Winpisinger of the Machinists, in that hearty, good-dose-of-castor-oil style (quoted, with much of what follows, from Byron E. Calame's labor column in the *Wall Street Journal* of February 26, 1973). "The better the wage, the greater the job satisfaction." In doubt, meany reaches back for Gompers' simple slogan "more." And a bluff, no-nonsense approach to social engineering always goes down well with the boys.

Faced with the looming threat of job enrichment, the gross spokesman will even deny that there is such a thing as worker discontent. The generally enlightened Leonard Woodcock of the UAW lashes out at the trusty old target, "elitist academics," for talking "a lot of nonsense about job enrichment," while Professor Irving Kristol accuses the social scientists of practically inventing the problem. (When the elitists are invoked, Labor is down to its last argument.)

Now while I yield to just about everyone in my respect for social scientists in bulk, there really is such a thing as blue-collar blues, as bad as ever and less passive in expression, and meany knows it. "There is something there and we need to know more about it," Jacob Clayman, head of the AFL-CIO Industrial Union Department, says cautiously. Unfortunately, most of the ideas for job enrichment have come from management, and are automatically suspect. Job enrichment is just "a stopwatch in sheep's clothing," says Winpisinger. An enriched worker is tempted to overproduce. And management, in sheep's clothing, may ask him to do two or three jobs for the sake of "variety" and personality development, while quietly cutting down staff. Whatever one may think about unions, there really is a big bad wolf out there.

Management is certainly not to be trusted single-handed with the problem. But again, Labor is slow with its own ideas. Older workers, of the kind the leaders are most in touch with, don't want job enrichment anyway. It's just a distraction in their anesthetic rounds. More profoundly, job enrichment "divides the worker and his union," as another gross spokesman puts it. If management begins "designing" the job and rearranging assignments, the worker begins to look to management for his signals, and his own union sinks into shadow. In some cases, he may even cross crafts, and do work proper to another union altogether, in which case paying dues and going to meetings becomes utterly onerous and pointless. The worker's perennial fear of being sold out by his leadership is matched here by the leadership's fear of losing him.

And meany knows all this too. His natural mode of operation is to oppose the new with low growls until compromise is reached, and then to proclaim it as if he'd invented it. Woodcock has already professed a grudging willingness to take part in enrichment experiments, and as autos go, so goes America. If the workers want job enrichment, they'll get it eventually; but the leaders naturally would like to seem to have gotten it for them. If management ever begins to look like the worker's best friend, the unions have had it (and so, eventually, have the workers).

Has the blue-collar worker also undergone some great upheaval in character that makes him different in kind from his old man? It was fashionable a few years ago to say that he had entered the middle class, or was just about to. Now you'll hear that he's taken his six-pack to Gross Pointe and set up a working-class life-style there. (As a six-pack man myself, I sometimes think this bit of symbolism is overdone.) If "middle-class" means the high incomes that the loftiest unions pull down, then it's true that most other union workers are nowhere near it yet (and a small union is never more on its own from the movement than when it's bargaining); but if it means tea sets in Grosse Pointe, we're talking fashion and not some deep-set historical pattern. These matters of style fluctuate inconsequentially, and whatever is true today won't be true tomorrow. The image of the hardhat looking down from a girder has had a big run in TV commercials, and may have affected the reality. And it certainly has its attractions after an overdose of Abbie Hoffman. But the image of the hard-hat at home is less sharp and compelling. Ethnic rediscovery has not yet won out over the Sears Roebuck décor and the five-hour-a-night television set. (Open a Polish folk center and see.) The infatuation with hard-hats is actually a gesture without cultural soil. Unionized teachers and civil servants outnumber builders by a considerable degree, but that man on the girder has the faded glamour of a Western hero.

What may be much more significant is that the white-collar unions are growing in number while some of the old blue-collars are shrinking. This could affect the national profile of Labor and, more immediately, the power balance on the Executive Council. The likes of Joe Beirne of the Communications Workers and Jerry Wurf of the Municipal Employees have enough members to make a tiny stir up there, and as we'll see in a moment, they may have already done so. Since these unions tend to be more liberal and democratic than most, their influence on the Council may filter down to other unions where it's needed. The Department of Labor may profit from a new ventriloquist. Who knows? The building trades may even cease to be called the lords of the union movement someday, though I doubt it. (The builders have the most intimate links with politicians and will always make out OK.)

Whatever happens up there, most blue-collar workers are likely not to care too much. They live further from the job than their forefathers and have more to do in the evenings. I suspect the real secret of the blue-collar worker lurks in the tube, along with all our secrets. Television watching is the premier social fact of our time, and I don't see why workers should be spared it. According to Nicholas Johnson of the FCC, "By 1969, over 95 percent of the nation's households spent more than one-fourth of their waking hours in rapt attention before the images on their television screens." And "the average child of eighteen has spent nearly 25,000 hours in front of the television set, and has seen approximately 350,000 commercials." (*How to Talk Back to Your Television Set,* Atlantic–Little, Brown, 1970.) Anyway, many union meeting halls are languishing right now like Broadway theaters. Some black leaders decided to go it alone on the McGovern campaign, and to remain bonded thereafter to deal with black union interest— but there is no evidence that more blacks are going to meetings. Twenty percent of union workers are women, but they race each other back to their TV's as fast as anyone else. If union democracy falters, it will be partly from worker apathy.

Or is apathy the word? The above-mentioned Mr. Winpisinger, who snorts at job enrichment, concedes "the rising level of contract rejections and the growing number of defeats suffered by long-established business representatives and officers in union elections." The workers may be bored with meany and the good-old-boy superstructure, but they're not necessarily bored with the actual gristle of unionism, the improvement of job conditions, and the right somehow to impose themselves on their work. If they can't do this through their appointed leaders, and if they can't always be bothered to go to meetings, they may do it themselves anyway, and on the job. Figures on minor job sabotage are hard to obtain, and it could be that they are a constant like suicide. But there's an unsettling amount of it right now. Otherwise, small spontaneous strikes on the local level may be the thing to watch—especially if the national organizations are thinking of abandoning the strike altogether.

Change is often more talked about (and feared) than practiced, and more apparent than real. Take the great American sport of collective bargaining. The early history of this sounds somewhat like the early days of pro football, with teams like the Canton Bulldogs gloomily slugging it out in the mud. Now the negotiators are urbane professionals who know each other's tricks by heart ("You could play a record from last year," says Bert Powers) and who "know that an agreement must be reached," as negotiator

Ted Kheel puts it. In fact, the two sides now understand each other's interests so well that people are beginning to talk.

Still, it all comes down to a cool mind and a hard bottom. Powers, who nearly struck the New York *Times* in the spring of 1973, is acknowledged king of the latter. He once sat twenty-seven hours at a stretch, and, when necessary, takes catnaps under a blanket of whatever newspapers are still left in New York. "They all come in like lions," he says. "You can't settle anything in the first couple of hours." I asked if his eyes ever glazed over or if boredom crept in, and he seemed amused by the question. Whatever errors of judgment might be coaxed out by ennui will not come from him. ("If you snooze, you lose," says Gomer Goins of the G.M. bargaining team.) Powers and Kheel are the most patient-*looking* men I've ever seen outside of Lord's Cricket Ground.

Although computers might be expected someday soon to bargain directly with each other, producing exquisitely nuanced solutions, Powers and Kheel are as scornful of this as only professionals can be. Kheel in particular stresses intuition, a sense of the possible, which may turn up like a gift for music in any kid from the shop, and be equally missing from a well-known leader. The best bargainer Kheel ever met was John Gordy of the Detroit Lions, who dabbled in it for a year or two and then quit. "No scruples at all," said Kheel admiringly. The worst bargainer? He grinned. Obviously, he wouldn't want to put such a one out of business.

The trouble with negotiators, as with lawyers and

other games players, is that their sport can become the whole world to them. Kheel, for instance, relishes strikes. They are the mustard of his profession, bracing for all concerned, especially the union. A strike may be the only time the rank and file gets to learn union business. And the leader becomes most fully himself. Besides, bargaining without strikes is like a gun without bullets. Both he and Powers throw up their hands in horror at the thought of outside arbitration. How could an outsider have that sense of music, for hitting the curve, that the kid in the shop has? "I don't worry about the money," says Powers. "You know at once how much they've got. It's the other things." The artist plays pension plans against overtime and work safety and comes out with a contract that is often a genuine original.

With these pros, to call in outside arbitration would be like taking away their ball. Maybe fortunately for the public, it isn't Meany's ball. Remember—"He never led a strike. His rise was purely political." He says now that strikes are almost obsolete and has declared himself in favor of third-party arbitration of a nonbinding sort: another kind of gun without bullets, perhaps.

If Labor wants to lose its abrasive image, Meany is obviously right. As A. J. Liebling pointed out years ago, unions always "demand," while employers "offer" —so that bad publicity is built into even neutral descriptions of strikes. And labor leaders are quick to tell you that newspaper publishers are seldom neutral: by temperament Republican, self-made, dogmatic at table, they are the least union-minded of employers. "You never even get to meet them," says Powers. "They all use agents." Powers adds, interestingly, that TV news may be fairer than newspapers about strikes of all sorts.

Besides the specific irritations of strikes, which seem to drill at each nerve in the body in turn—bad phone service today, long hikes in the snow tomorrow —there is the general sense of threat, as one stage villain replaces another on the evening news, growling his demands.

One anti-Labor result of frequent strikes is that the nonunionized poor are reminded of how little they themselves make. A union is required, by the nature of the game, to ask for much more than it gets, and that's the figure that sticks in the head and the craw. "Did you see the cement workers are asking for such-and-such? Why, Ph.D.'s don't get that much." Neither do cement workers, but the damage is done.

Another result is that the labor-costs component in inflation is always being flashed before the public eye, while the head of G.M. takes his money home quietly. A recent survey of union members shows that 61 percent of *them* believe that excessive union demands are the major cause of inflation. After all, they're consumers themselves half the time, and they are tired of wiping out each other's raises methodically. The have-not unions keep an especially beady eye on the have unions, of which Mr. Meany's pet building trades unions are outstanding—although they may find their hands full competing with the new assembly-line low-cost housing outfits. Workers who have scraped up enough for a house in the suburbs are not happy to learn why they can't afford it after all, or why they can't get a plumber either. Ownership makes capitalists of us all, and as workers move up the pay scale, they find themselves dealing with more and more unions from a quasi-managerial position, which snarls up the class war as it is always being snarled up in this country.

Arbitration would presumably hush some of this up. It would take some glory from the swashbuckling leaders, but much pressure too: they wouldn't have to bargain for their pants anymore, but could say to their membership in effect, "They made me sign," and then curse the arbitration law, instead of management.

According to the anti-arbitrationists, such shadow-boxing would be even more artificial than Mike Quill's orchestrated tantrums. The leaders under this arrangement would scarcely be accountable to their members at all. They could come out of the back room with whatever deal they liked, blaming it all on the other parties (who would do the same). The workers' latent fear of being sold out to the boss would presumably intensify, and they would either lose interest or start organizing again on lower levels against the whole superstructure.

No wonder Meany hedged the arbitration suggestion with nullifying restrictions. Still, the proposal is there, and has been taken up by other leaders, such as I. W. Abel, in Steel, a symbol of the new syndicalism—an alliance between the bigs of Labor, business, and government against the smaller versions of each. If the AFL-CIO doesn't know that that's what Nixon has been up to, they haven't been paying attention.

If Labor gives up the strike, bargaining will become one more empty ritual, like tossing the coin at football games. And one must assume that it would fix the status of have and have-not unions about as is, screwing them even more definitively than Phase 2 did. It would deal a death blow to union democracy. Who would bother to go to meetings anymore? And it would cement the partnership between Labor and management: meanyism triumphant. As in *Animal Farm,* the pigs at the bargaining table would look just like the people.

Some believe they already do. In his book *The Company and the Union* (Knopf, 1973), about the 1970 G.M. strike, William Serrin quotes a black auto worker as saying, "The union and the company, they're more or less partners." That is, they're in business to perpetuate each other. It is hard to buy this in relation to a sixty-seven-day strike that must have hurt somebody. In fact, the UAW had to take out a mortgage with the Teamsters afterwards. But if collusion can be suspected in a crippling strike, imagine what would be suspected of arbitration.

It seems perverse to miss the old-fashioned strike— as soon miss leprosy—but it is the one earnest of intent that everyone accepts (except the cynics who say that business uses strikes to raise prices twice as much as necessary) and it may just possibly be on the way out. Recently, I. W. Abel agreed with ten major steel companies on an experimental "no strike" guarantee plan, allegedly to head off the stockpiling that can occur when a strike is feared. Steel is an important indicator, being a union that can close down a whole industry and adjoining industries. If wages there are decided by prearranged slide rule, it might be contagious. The strike-happy railroad unions have also agreed to binding arbitration, and if those old feather-bedders can do it, anybody can.

For the plaintiff, it can be pointed out that these are both special cases. Steel loses millions by stockpiling and hedge-buying every time a strike is feared, and those millions come out of the workers' hides one way or another—if only when foreign companies take advantage of our padded prices. "You can't stockpile a hemline" is the word from the garment workers, and you can't stockpile teaching or hospital care either. The gnat-bite municipal strikes will be with us the longest.

Heady prophecies were made, in the wake of Steel's decision, that there would be no more nationwide emergency strikes ever again, but this could be as premature as that "generation of peace" we were going to get. Rubber and Autos have turned down arbitration cold, possibly to see how Steel makes out, more likely because they're not interested, and one awaits their new contracts this year with interest, not to say panic. Finally, Steel has a singularly autocratic boss in Abel, and it is not clear that a more turbulent membership would sit still for arbitration just yet.

The railroad workers accepted arbitration simply because they feared legislation—that old nemesis—which would ban nationwide transit strikes altogether. This still seems the most likely way for arbitration to arrive, if it does: from above. Meanwhile, the public can content itself with the words of Willard Wirtz, former Secretary of Labor: "Sometimes a bad settlement hurts the public worse than a strike." An agreement to soak the consumer hurts worse than a strike, though you can't see it. And workers, who double as members of the public, have several reasons to view the death of the strike with caution, even though it would make them a heck of a lot more popular in the short run.

The new bipartisanship that meany has worked out is a hoary political device, half buried in claptrap. His dynamic progressive centerism still depends squarely on the same liberal sentimentality he sneers at. Americans like a roughhewn labor leader with all his sins better than a smooth manager, even when both are up to the same tricks. So as long as he stays roughhewn (and meany is great at this as seen above), his left is safe enough. We may frown over Big Labor, but we don't sick Ralph Nader on it or run candidates against it. McGovern murmured something about running against an abstract called Big Labor but nobody picked it up, and before you knew it George was promising to remove all wage and price controls in ninety days—more than even Meany asked. (Parson George was a great one for going the extra mile.)

And if all else fails with the middle-class Left, the nonquestion of party affiliation can always be summoned once again. "The Executive Council may be moving left," a friendly intellectual and labor expert told me recently. Why? Because Joe Beirne of the Communications Workers, a rabid hawk, had recently changed feathers and challenged Meany over his Vietnam War position. The thing to note about this is that the war was virtually over, so the challenge was purely academic. Beirne was also accusing Meany of deserting the Democratic Party in the last election— but the election is over too. I asked my friend if any issue of present substance was involved and he said he couldn't think of any offhand.

Being liberal over dead questions is a perfect way to keep the Left happy. And the late war still serves beautifully for empty displays of independence. To see how much it really means to Meany, observe that Vic Gotbaum felt quite free to oppose the boss of bosses on it—he went for McGovern—but has not felt free to support Jim Morissey's union-democracy challenge, which is a real issue.

Since Beirne's overnight conversion to peace has to be suspect, one must assume he was reaching for the support Meany had lost, without actually giving it anything. This may be interesting in terms of Meany's power on the Council—Beirne can perhaps hope for enough support from Jerry Wurf and Paul Jennings of the Electricians to challenge the king— but not so far, in terms of real political trends. Meany may be threatened, but meany lives on. (In fairness to my informant, a wise man, it would probably make a difference if Meany's successor turns out to be one of the comparative liberals on the Council. But it's rather like assuming that a Humphrey will be better than an LBJ. Until liberal labor leaders debate something more vibrant than the last war, we can't guess what they would do to alter the course of Labor. And as long as intellectuals equate Democratic Party affiliation with the Left, they won't really have to do anything.)

With the Left rumbling softly but safe for now, Meany has been free to browse to his right and has done so. Big companies deal more comfortably with big unions anyway. It's tidier and possibly even cheaper. Fewer strikes mean fewer unions playing leapfrog for wage increases. For a politician, it means one box of cigars to give instead of twenty, one deal, one friend. The Right has no reason to dislike big unions. With their bureaucratic accountants and economic advisers, the big labor unions are more sophisticated and aware of the national interest than are the little wildcat outfits.

Yet, unless they are consummate playactors, I have to believe that Labor people found the alliance with Nixon distasteful even before Watergate exploded; a sign of weakness, not strength. Meany would prefer a Democratic Party to his taste, and he continues to make the old partisan noises. Peter Brennan had not been Labor Secretary for long before Meany attacked him for selling out to the Nixon Administration on minimum wage legislation. And, sincere or no, it is the kind of thing Meany has to do if he values his left base at all.

Perhaps as liberals grow older and are replaced (or not replaced), that base could slide away anyhow, leaving meany alone with his new friends and making Labor officially rightist for the first time, though hardly in control of the GOP. Young lefties may, in turn, celebrate the old Wobbly virtues of Cesar Chavez and the crusading union democrats, and a new movement might conceivably be born under the old one. But with the new politics in its current shell shock, with Chavez on the ropes and the union democrats scrambling for crumbs, it seems pretty remote right now. With meany relatively secure for this year at least, we can take one last look at him in his splendid immobility. For all its faults, the AFL-CIO remains a relatively liberal influence in a business society: it does, for whatever reason, support social legislation, and it has sufficient economic sophistication not to rip off the public unnecessarily. Its major defect is that if it decides to live in a world of its own, no one can stop it.

In the matter of corruption, the AFL-CIO may be no worse than the candlestick makers; but unfortunately their only method of dealing with it seems to be expulsion, and their No. 1 Horrible Example, the Teamsters, has flourished exceedingly well on its own. Freed from AFL-CIO jurisdictional taboos, the Teamsters now prowl the workworld like a tomcat, unionizing everything that isn't nailed down and ironically, advancing the Wobbly ideal of One Big Union much more than the staid old AFL is doing.

The Teamsters are the professional bad boys of American Labor and their treatment of Chavez in the California grape and produce fields (signing a contract without figures on it to beat him out) was breathtaking. Yet they also have some of the best and liveliest of locals, especially on the West Coast and St.

Louis, along with the crookedest, in (surprise) New Jersey. Their power is one of the unknowns in the equation; Nixon thinks enough of it to court them every bit as industriously as he courts Meany. And he may know something. Theoretically, they, of all unions, can paralyze the nation, just by tying up road cargo. Yet they have refrained so far from national strikes, maybe being too rich to need them.

The Auto Workers, or professional good guys, are another unknown. If they come back to the AFL-CIO, they will presumably help democratize it, as they helped Arnold Miller with the Mine Workers, besides rolling Labor's political clout back into one fist. But outside of the occasional trip to Miami, it's hard to see what's in it for Leonard Woodcock. His dues would be close to one million a year—a heavy price to pay for agreeing with meany and sharing his lobbyist—and educated opinion has it that he probably won't go back if Meany is replaced by another building tradesman. (A merger with the Machinists is a possible alternative, which would give us yet another unknown, and an interesting one.)

All my life I've been hearing that Labor is at the crossroads, that it's finally gotten too big for us and must be definitively crushed. The easy thing now, as our President might say, is to announce a Turning Point and say that the crossroads are here. But neither the President nor I ever choose the easy thing. Labor hears those voices too, and knows that when they grow too loud, punitive legislation is on its way. (Labor tries fitfully not to pass this irritation line.) The next wave of resentment may always be the last.

THREE MOBS: LABOR, CHURCH AND MAFIA

In 1973, for instance there was ominous talk about major contracts coming up that would balloon prices and beggar us all. Yet the unions involved proved to be the soul of reasonableness, even considering dreaded arbitration, as we've seen. Also, in regard to wage-price controls, meany has been as cooperative as his role permits while fulminating for the record about fat-cats and capital gains. The real menace, if one has to have one, is not big unionism itself, but the impressment of its leaders into an Establishment troika with business and government, planning the economy from above. In this arrangement, Labor would not be the strong partner. Its so-called power is largely defensive anyway. In fact, it has yet to prove it can flourish full force in a time of peace and plenty, or, more specifically, that it can cope with the multi-national companies, or with the superdeals of the superpowers, business and government respectively doing their stuff. Labor may feel itself lucky to be let into the troika at all if this keeps up.

The logical alternative would seem to be a growth in international unionism—"Workers of the world unite" is hardly Meany's favorite slogan, but if capital can mate anywhere at will, maybe the work force can get together at least a little. And on the home front, some more conspicuous brotherhood wouldn't hurt. The widespread impression that Labor consists of aging white men guarding their gains may be an exaggeration verging on a libel: but it is widespread. And when blue-collar ethnics seem to be consistently at odds with the unskilled minorities, the worker as a political force is weakened. And no short-term bribe from any politician is worth that. Again, meany presumably knows all this. The AFL-CIO has excellent position papers on mergers and multinationals, and is theoretically enlightened about race and everything else there is to be enlightened about. Meanwhile, meany moves *slowly*.

Whatever prediction one makes must start with the understanding that if the old boys had their way, nothing would change at all. Compared with them, the Roman Catholic Curia is downright flighty. Changes are still more likely to come from outside—from the kindness of politicians, or from new styles in business, or from a new breed of worker. Predict those and you can predict meany a few feet behind, growling, opposing, accepting. Surviving.

THREE MOBS: LABOR, CHURCH AND MAFIA

AN AFL-CIO PRIMER

(This, and the following A Short Guide to Unionland, *were compiled and written by Judith Ramsey.)*

The AFL-CIO is a union of unions. Each of its 116 affiliates is autonomous, except for constitutional strictures with regard to corruption, discrimination, and Communism.

Policy in matters affecting the federation is made at biennial conventions at which each affiliate is represented in proportion to its membership. The convention also elects the president and secretary-treasurer, invariably George Meany, 78, and Lane Kirkland, 51. It also elects thirty-three vice presidents, most of them presidents of their own unions. Seven vice presidents come from the building trades. Implementation of policy is carried out by the AFL-CIO Executive Council, comprised of the above-mentioned officers. Only George Meany ($90,000 annually) and Lane Kirkland ($60,000) have salaried jobs; the others are paid by their union.

Then there are the departments and their directors. Alexander Barkan heads COPE, the Committee on Political Education, which pours millions of dollars and much manpower into the political campaigns of candidates supported by Labor. In 1972 COPE put $4 million into the congressional races but remained "neutral" on the presidency. Andrew Biemiller, the chief labor lobbyist on Capitol Hill, runs the department of legislation. Nathaniel Goldfinger, an economist, is in charge of the department of research and works with government officials on wage-price control matters. Jay Lovestone runs the department of foreign affairs, and Donald Slaiman the department of civil rights. There are others, but these are probably the most important.

For AFL-CIO affiliates with strong common interests there are six constitutional departments with their own officers, rules, and dues structures. The most important are Building and Construction, the Industrial Union, the Maritime Trades, and the Metal Trades. These departments, which are generally not answerable to the Executive Council, deal with matters of concern to their own constituency—for example, in the case of Metal Trades, the threat of companies that move their plants to foreign countries, thereby displacing American workers.

The same federation principle exists in microcosm on state and local levels, where central labor bodies are chartered by the AFL-CIO. The federations lobby for and implement legislative programs at the state level.

City and county central labor bodies unite the political efforts of local unions. However, the locals are not bound to affiliate with them. In fact, in certain areas the local central body is much more powerful than the state federation. This is certainly true in New York City, and in Cook County, Illinois.

THREE MOBS: LABOR, CHURCH AND MAFIA

A SHORT GUIDE TO UNIONLAND

Labor, unlike industry, still has its parochial side. The last *Who's Who in Labor* was published in 1946. Labor Department and AFL-CIO directories are not up to date, so dozens of phone calls had to be made to compile this roster. Responses were predictable. One Teamster official snarled: "Don't think you're doing us a favor putting us in your guide." (It never occurred to us.) And in this old boys' club where many of the most prominent members are over 70, union public relations types were often reluctant to reveal their bosses' ages.

The federal government lists more than 80 million Americans currently in the work force. Under 20 million—fewer than one out of every four—belong to trade unions. Of these, 13,600,000 are members of the 116 unions making up the American Federation of Labor and Congress of Industrial Organizations (AFL-CIO). Its members range from the Steelworkers with over a million members, to the Horseshoers with less than 350, to actors, barbers, teachers, policemen, carpenters, and people in almost every walk of life. Then there are the independent unions and employee organizations operating outside AFL-CIO jurisdiction, of which the Teamsters, Auto Workers, Mine Workers, and National Education Association are the largest.

Seventy-five percent of labor membership is concentrated in 10 large industrial states. There are more union members in New York than in 11 Southern states, including Texas.

Here is a partial listing of major unions and employee organizations and their leaders, those likely to have the greatest impact on your life:

BUILDING AND CONSTRUCTION

This industry does a $100-billion annual business, greater than auto and steel combined. The unionized work force is divided into 17 crafts and 10,000 locals —representing more than 3 million workers—who bargain with most of the nation's 870,000 contractors. About 500,000 construction workers are not union members.

United Brotherhood of Carpenters and Joiners of America

Mergers in recent years have increased membership to 825,000, incorporating many small locals, millwrights, pile drivers, millmen, lumber and saw mill operators, to name just a few. After a long dynastic reign, Maurice Hutcheson, who succeeded his father William as president, stepped down at age 74. The appointed president is William Siddell, 58—*not* Hutcheson's son. As with the Mafia, rumors of nepotism are sometimes exaggerated. The Carpenters are a stronghold of Republican unionism, with paradoxically socialist underpinnings in New York and Philadelphia.

THREE MOBS: LABOR, CHURCH AND MAFIA

International Union of Operating Engineers

Conservative, with some allegedly corrupt locals where payoffs and collusive deals are a way of life, this union wields a lot of power in the building trades. Its 400,000 members are engaged in all types of construction, from buildings to highways. Its president, Hunter P. Wharton, gets $75,000 a year, plus full expenses.

United Association of Journeymen and Apprentices of the Plumbing and Pipe Fitting Industry of the United States and Canada

The union where Meany germinated. The plumbers are predominantly a craft union with 90,000 of its 300,000 members in construction. The new president, Martin Ward, is progressive by building trade standards.

International Brotherhood of Painters and Allied Trades

The painters' union (250,000 members) is made up of autonomous locals; a few of them have been linked with kickbacks and payoffs. President Frank Raftery covets Meany's job, but insiders say this is a pipe dream.

International Association of Bridge, Structural and Ornamental Iron Workers

Among the most highly paid of the building trades union members, iron workers earn $10-$11 per hour. The membership is 177,000 members. President John H. Lyons, who represents the cleaner elements in the building trades, reportedly calls Negroes "niggers." If the building tradesmen and more conservative leaders in the AFL-CIO back him, he is a contender for Meany's job.

Laborers' International Union of North America

With about 80 percent of its 600,000 members employed in construction, this is one building trade union with substantial black membership—mostly in unskilled, low-paying jobs. Leadership in East Coast locals is primarily Italian, reportedly with some mob connections. President Peter Fosco, about 70, is an outspoken hawk even compared to other hard-line labor leaders. Several days after he received a "good citizen" award from the Nixon Administration, Fosco endorsed Nixon.

Sheet Metal Workers' International Association

Despite some reported petty corruption on the local level, this 150,000-member union is felt to be reasonably honest. Asked about the best way to become a union president, union president Eddie Carlough (39) replied: "Your rise in the Union is rapid when your father happens to be president." (He succeeded his father.) Carlough is acceptable to a large segment of the building trades although he is a man of progressive ideas. Despite long hair and mod attire, he is conceivably a dark-horse candidate for Meany's job.

International Brotherhood of Electrical Workers

A large craft and industrial union (980,000 members), the IBEW swings weight in the AFL-CIO

Building Trades Department largely because of the personal force of its secretary, Joseph Keenan (78, a former golfing companion of Meany's), who overshadows president Charles Pillard. Labor talk has it that Keenan now is out of favor with Meany, possibly because he supported McGovern. Treasurer Harry Van Arsdale (68) heads the million-member New York City Central Labor Council. He's so powerful that in 1962 he was able to get a 25-hour work week for his electricians, over the protests of JFK and Meany.

MANUFACTURING

United Automobile, Aerospace and Agricultural Implement Workers of America*

This union has maintained the democratic, progressive tradition associated with Walter Reuther. It pioneered and set standards for other industrial unions in negotiating contracts on matters beyond the traditional wage-hours haggle such as cost-of-living wage increases and health care benefits. Today its 1.4 million members are largely engaged in the powerful automotive industry, but also make agricultural implements and road equipment—in fact, everything from cradles to grave vaults. Having won worker benefits, union leaders are now concerned with growing worker unrest and the threat of foreign imports.

The union is also undergoing a leadership shakeup. When Reuther was killed in a plane crash,

*Indicates union which is not a member of AFL-CIO.

Leonard Woodcock (62) beat Doug Frazier, head of the Chrysler division, by one executive board vote, cast by Emil Mazey, secretary-treasurer, who is influential in top leadership. Operating in Reuther's shadow, Woodcock has never been a dynamic leader; what's more, he is now only a few years away from mandatory retirement. Union officials are already lining up. Apart from Frazier, potential contenders are Pat Greathouse, head of organizing activities and a vice president, and Irving Bluestone, head of the G.M. division.

United Steelworkers of America

With a membership of 1.4 million, the steel union always has been an important force in the labor movement. It has lost some clout recently because of competition from foreign imports, lack of modernization, and substitutes for steel in many products. President I. W. Abel (64) used to be touted as a likely successor to Meany, but the fact that he's near retirement age probably rules him out. On the other hand, this rules out almost all the other candidates too. Abel is moving closer to cooperation with management. The Steelworkers and U.S. Steel jointly sponsored the film *Where's Joe?*, with menacing shots of Asian and German workers, proclaiming the threat of foreign imports and urging greater productivity at home.

United Mine Workers*

It took three murders (UMW executive board member Jock Yablonski and his wife and daughter in

THREE MOBS: LABOR, CHURCH AND MAFIA

1969) and costly Labor Department intervention to get a fair election, in which 49-year-old Arnold Miller, a disabled miner from West Virginia, wrested control of the UMW from Tony Boyle (70). It may be the first victory of a dissident rank-and-file leader over any union's incumbent president in recent years. Boyle, who took office in 1963, continued John L. Lewis' policies of flagrant paternalism, nepotism, and worse, without Lewis' compensatory vision. Boyle is faced with a prison sentence for making illegal political campaign contributions and has been implicated in the Yablonski murders. Miller began his presidency of the 207,000-member union (including pensioners) by trimming costs—including his own salary.

International Union of Electrical, Radio and Machine Workers

This 285,000-member union is in trouble. Major employers—such as Westinghouse, General Electric, Motorola, and Singer—have moved many plants overseas. It now bargains collectively with its long-term arch enemy, the United Electrical Workers (see below). President Paul Jennings defeated former president James Carey in a palace revolution with the help of Meany, who reportedly dislikes Carey and wanted to bump him from the AFL-CIO Executive Council.

United Electrical, Radio and Machine Workers of America*

Left of left by Labor's standards, the 165,000-member UE was ousted from the CIO in 1949 during the McCarthy anti-Communist era. Its current president, Albert Fitzgerald (65), and secretary-treasurer James Matles have been outspoken antiwar critics.

United Rubber, Cork, Linoleum and Plastic Workers of America

The threat of foreign imports is a small but real problem. Worker unrest is high; most of the 200,000 members are paid a basic wage plus piecework incentive (so much per tire, for example), an exhausting way to earn. They are pressing for earlier retirement and bigger pensions. President Peter Bommarito, a decent but not decisive man, is in trouble. The rubber contract he negotiated was rejected by big Goodyear Local 2 in Akron, Ohio, and subsequently by the Goodrich workers, who went on nationwide strike.

International Association of Machinists and Aerospace Workers

Originally a railroad craft union, it has since shifted to aerospace. With the loss of many aerospace and defense contracts following the winding down of the war and many job layoffs, membership dropped slightly from over a million to 927,000. President Floyd Smith, only a couple of years from mandatory retirement, is likely to be replaced by William Winpisinger, general vice president. The union is working closely with the UAW on political and economic issues. And there's talk of merger, which would make it the largest American union.

International Ladies' Garment Workers' Union

The leaders of this union have long held that job

security is predicated upon survival of the industry, and have therefore been more open to automation and job cutbacks than some other unions. Although it represents an industry employing women (80%), many of whom are black or Puerto Rican, the ILGWU has few women, blacks, and Puerto Ricans in prominent positions. Current president is Louis Stulberg (72). The man slated to replace Stulberg is Sol Chaiken (55). Asked to name the labor movement's leading philosopher, education director Gus Tyler (61) said "Me" with a grin.

Amalgamated Clothing Workers of America

Last year Jacob Potofsky finally stepped down at 78, turning the presidency over to Murray Finley. The 375,000-member union has been locked in a bitter strike with Farah, manufacturer of work pants and inexpensive slacks, which maintains plants in the southwestern United States, employing Chicanos at low wages. The clothing workers vow either to win their strike or destroy Farah. Both the Amalgamated Clothing and ILGWU workers face stiff competition from foreign-made goods.

TRANSPORTATION

International Brotherhood of Teamsters, Chauffeurs, Warehousemen and Helpers of America*

The Teamsters were thrown out of the old AFL in 1955 for corruption when president Dave Beck was exposed as an embezzler. James Hoffa took over and negotiated excellent contracts for his elite members, the more than 100,000 over-the-road truckers. Non-truckers, such as laborers and warehouse people, consistently got inferior contracts. Graft and corruption flourished, and mob ties have been alleged in most big cities. However, West Coast locals under the leadership of regional director Elinar Mohn and St. Louis locals headed by the once powerful Harold Gibbons are reputed to be relatively honest unions. In 1972 they were among McGovern's staunchest supporters. Their support of Teamster attempts to break Cesar Chavez indicates the complexity of the union's power politics.

When Hoffa was jailed for misappropriation of funds, Frank Fitzsimmons took over and reactivated the old baronies, consolidating his position with business agents and regional directors. His salary is $125,000; he is reported to have a fleet of Cadillacs and a jet plane at his disposal. (By contrast, Cesar Chavez' salary is $5144.) Fitzsimmons has one big worry: Hoffa may try to stage a comeback, and he is very popular with members.

Free of AFL-CIO jurisdictional strictures, the Teamsters have gobbled up small locals all over the country, bringing membership to over 2 million.

Fitzsimmons is now the only labor leader with easy access to the White House. In the past five years, the Teamsters have been charged with more Landrum-Griffin violations than all other unions combined, but to date have escaped any serious consequences.

National Maritime Union of America

Dwindling membership (down to 50,000), rising

costs, and decline of the U.S. Merchant Marine have meant trouble for the NMU, which pays a very large percentage of its per capita dues to elected officials. After a long rule of 36 years, former president Joseph Curran retired with a royal pension, $55,000 annual pension for life, which is now in litigation. Their membership is comprised mainly of unlicensed seamen and Panamanian workers.

Seafarers' International Union of North America

Another union with dwindling membership (now 80,000), its remaining strength is largely its effective and popular president Paul Hall, 58. He heads the AFL-CIO Maritime Trades Department, is a friend of Meany's, but also (at times) champion of the underdog. After blasting Chavez at an AFL-CIO Executive Council meeting for being erratic and irresponsible (supporting the Black Panthers, for one thing), he gave a rousing pitch for the support of Chavez' union, personally pledging $25,000 and muscle from the Seafarers. Hall has to be considered a potential successor to Meany; he gets along well with the building tradesmen.

Brotherhood of Railway, Airline and Steamship Clerks, Freight Handlers, Express and Station Employees

This 150,000-member union has lost out in recent years. The bankruptcy of major railroads has meant job layoffs, and the airlines have proved stubborn bargainers.

International Longshoremen's Association

Led by flag-waving, right-wing Thomas Gleason

(72), this 115,000-member East Coast union was once expelled from the AFL-CIO for being racketeer-dominated.

International Longshoremen's and Warehousemen's Union*

Ousted from the CIO in 1949 during Red-baiting days under the individualistic and concerned leadership of Harry Bridges—a pre-New Deal leftist—this union overcame automation of the docks. Bridges is still in charge, despite repeated attempts by the government to deport him. At their convention this spring, the 55,000-member union decided against continuing merger talks with the Teamsters.

PUBLIC EMPLOYEES AND SERVICE WORKERS

Public employees are not protected by labor legislation on the state and federal levels. These unions, therefore, are prone to strikes, nearly always illegal, which irritate the public to madness.

American Federation of State, County and Municipal Employees

The fifth largest and fastest-growing union (average may be better than 1000 new members a week), these 612,000 workers include engineers, medical technicians, zoo keepers, scientists, pothole patchers, and policemen. Contrary to general belief, roughly 60 percent of the members are blue-collar workers. Membership is one-third black and one-third female. Members are scattered throughout the country, but most are concentrated in the Northeast and Midwest. An offshoot of the La Follette administration in Wisconsin in the early 1930s, AFSCME has consistently been one of the most progressive and militant unions in the AFL-CIO. It was one of the first to endorse McGovern.

President Jerry Wurf, 53, a capable leader, is regarded as a maverick with a fast mouth and plenty of admirers and critics. He is quick to admit that his chances for Meany's job are very, very slim. "If it were reasonable to be ambitious for it, I would be ambitious." Secretary-treasurer Bill Lucy is 39 and black. In New York, Vic Gotbaum heads up politically active District 37, which invariably backs Democratic reform candidates. The district's associate director is 45-year-old Lillian Roberts, a very able black. The State and County union has about 150,000 members in health services.

American Federation of Government Employees

Since the Kennedy executive order (10988) in 1961 enabling federal employees legally to join unions, this one has grown rapidly. Responsive largely to employees in defense and Pentagon installations, the 300,000-member union has provoked criticism from HEW, OEO, and HUD workers who are pushing for collective bargaining. Its president John Griner became ill and recently was replaced by Clyde Webber. Despite rapid growth, it has financial problems. Griner was voted down at the convention when he tried to put through a per capita dues increase. The opposition is confused, and cannot unify behind a single program or candidate.

American Postal Workers Union

Although their destinies are irrevocably tied together, the 285,000 members of the Postal Workers and the Letter Carriers (see below) can't solve differences. So the Postal Workers and Letter Carriers are discussing merger with the Communications Workers instead. In 1970 the postal service became a private operation. President Francis Filbey is having a hard time; several smaller postal unions merged in the late 1960s, and the various factions have never been united.

National Association of Letter Carriers of the U.S.A.

Same problems. President James H. Rademacher is a Nixon man. Membership: 220,000.

Fraternal Order of Police*

An employee organization of about 100,000 members with no national power. Headquarters in Cleveland. There is no single big police organization in the nation. Some police belong to the State, County and Municipal Employees, others to the Teamsters; still others have organized (as in New York) in Benevolent Order of Police groups.

American Federation of Teachers

The second fastest-growing union in the nation, the AFT's 380,000 members are not evenly distributed throughout the country; half of them are in New York

State, about a third in New York City. That's one reason why Albert Shanker, 44, head of United Federation of Teachers in New York, and vice president of New York State United Teachers, is more powerful than 58-year-old AFT president Dave Selden. Shanker rode to fame during the Ocean Hill-Brownsville controversy on school decentralization and aspires to a place on the AFL-CIO Executive Council, which would be unique for the head of a local—if he remains that. Shanker is extraordinarily ambitious, on good terms with Peter Brennan and Harry Van Arsdale, and reportedly aspires to Meany's job—though as one union leader put it, "Those guys'll never let a teacher run them."

National Education Association*

With its membership of 1.2 million, the NEA is larger than the AFT. The latter wants a merger, but the NEA is divided. Some of its members favor merger, others want it but without AFL-CIO affiliation, still others—primarily in the South—want to stay independent. A merger within AFL-CIO would make them the largest union in the federation. The sensitive question is who would be on top. The odds favor Shanker over any NEA president, if only because the latter has just a one-year term of office. The current one is Catharine Barrett.

International Association of Fire Fighters

One of the more conservative unions in the field, its 165,000 members are mostly white. (In several big cities black firemen are not hired.) For what it's worth, president W. Howard McClennan is the only union president who picked up his own phone when we called.

SERVICE UNIONS

Service Employees' International Union

Made up of building service employees and custodial and maintenance workers, the 480,000-member Service Employees' has branched out to include a variety of service industries—from redcaps and skycaps to hospital workers. President George Hardy, 58, comes from San Francisco in a state where the union is very strong.

Retail Clerks International Association

This 400,000-member union has grown rapidly in recent years, organizing low-paid workers in supermarkets and retail stores. President James Housewright has shown moderately progressive leadership.

Retail, Wholesale and Department Store Union

Organizing a variety of industries in retail and wholesale trades, this 150,000-member union has an affiliate—Local 1199, Drug and Hospital Union. 1199 has sparked the formation of a 900,000-member national union of hospital and nursing-home employees, a division of RWDSU, and the name of 1199 became a symbol—rare for a local. The Hospital Union—whose membership is predominantly black and Puerto Rican women—has organized in New York, Philadelphia, Boston, and Baltimore. 1199 president in New York,

THREE MOBS: LABOR, CHURCH AND MAFIA

Leon Davis, a benign, rabbinical figure, has become a labor hero to many black workers and middle-class liberals alike.

Hotel and Restaurant Employees and Bartenders International Union

Rising food costs affect these workers' wages; they are in for a hard time. Membership: 450,000.

MISCELLANEOUS UNIONS

Amalgamated Meat Cutters and Butcher Workmen of North America

An amalgam of 550,000 workers, the Meat Cutters and Butcher Workmen absorbed the smaller packinghouse workers' union. These days a supermarket is more likely to hire meat cutters than skilled butchers. A few New York locals have been linked with payoffs. On the national scene secretary-treasurer Pat Gorman (80), an old-time socialist and no friend of Meany's, overshadows union president Joseph Belsky.

Communications Workers of America

For many years this was a company union, doing what was good for Ma Bell. Today it is more worker-oriented, with 550,000 members primarily in telephone and electronics as well as some hospital workers. President Joseph Beirne, 62—erratic, first a vigorous hawk, then supporter of McGovern—may have had his last hurrah. He was publicly humiliated by Meany at last year's AFL-CIO convention in Florida, thereby wiping out his chances to succeed Meany.

Graphic Arts International Union

An amalgam of lithographers, photoengravers, and bookbinders, this 120,000-member union has been absorbing craft unions threatened by automation. President Ken Brown has been talking merger with the American Newspaper Guild.

International Typographical Union

An old craft union, it vigorously resisted automation and modern technology—and has paid a high price for its intransigence. Its strikes helped put a number of newspapers out of business. It is best known on the local level—particularly in New York City, where Bert Powers, president of Local 6, keeps everyone quaking when newspaper contracts run out. Membership: 112,000.

United Farm Workers

The survival of this 40,000-member union is in doubt. Labor's dispossessed, the Farm Workers triumphed in organizing migrant grape and lettuce pickers—primarily Chicano and Filipino workers—through the successful use of the strike and grape boycott, with nationwide liberal support. The Farm Workers brought the pickers a hiring hall and many fringe benefits. Then in the spring of 1973, just when the table grape contracts were about to expire, the Teamsters moved in and persuaded growers to sign with them. Immediately the United Farm Workers struck all the growers who signed a labor agreement with the Teamsters.

With fresh AFL-CIO support of $1.6 million, the UFW is preparing for a long hard fight and another grape boycott. President Cesar Chavez, himself a former migrant worker with only a seventh-grade education, has to cope with issues such as separate rest rooms and child labor that other unions consider part of the Stone Age.

II

America's Catholics

The decline of the American Catholic Church in the late Sixties has become a statistician's plaything, as the empty pew is weighted against the growth of Real Concern. Thus: the sprawling seminaries of the Fifties may be ghost towns—but we are all priests now. Likewise, the swollen churches can't meet their mortgages—but then, our life is our prayer. That kind of argument. The decline of a state of mind is hard to chart and I leave it to the professionals (anything so unanswerable must have money in it). But for those of us who lived through it, the physical fact itself, and the loss of institutional confidence that went with it, formed a psychic event so unmistakably spectacular that we felt as if our tripes had been removed by sleight of hand. The Church was still standing solid as the post office in, say, 1966; the Vatican Council had been weathered—better than weathered. In fact, the first death spasm looked like a little dance step. (The first half hour of freedom is always the best: we would be *better* Catholics without coercion.) And then it was gone.

THREE MOBS: LABOR, CHURCH AND MAFIA

That Church, anyway: the Catholic Church of America, walled off from its enemies by airtight womb to tomb education: Alcatraz, the Rock, very hard to leave. The Jesuits had been given boys not just till they were seven but till they were thirty-seven, and had used every minute of it: yet suddenly ex-Jesuits were pouring out in beards and atrocious sports shirts. Can one be un-brainwashed? Or was the brainwashing as superficial as most education?

Even if, as some die-hards maintain, it was only a flight of the liberals,[1] who characteristically declared the joint closed the moment they left, it was amazing enough. Habits of a lifetime (and even liberals have habits) fell like dominoes. The fatal glass of beer theory we'd been warned about came true. Prayers, fasts, even Sunday mass itself came off in one piece. And of course it wasn't just liberals—who after all want to believe so much they'll do anything to make the Church believable, even deface it if necessary—but the well-drilled mob in the middle. God's foot soldiers, the middle-aged middle-class parishioners, downed rosaries and defected in thousands to the prevailing life-styles, adopting even this barbarous word. (*Modus vivendi* isn't good enough any more.) De-

---

[1] Liberal Catholic is a hopelessly untechnical term, like liberal anything else. In a sense, a traditionalist like John Henry Newman was a liberal because he believed in the growth and development of doctrine, while the reformer Hans Küng is a conservative because he wants to return *holus bolus* to the practices of the early Church. So too, in politics, Barry Goldwater can accept the twentieth century more easily than Eugene McCarthy. Here I use the words simply as indexes of temperament: the liberal emphasizing the living (thus changing) Church, the conservative stressing Peter's Rock—without whose solidity he finds life and change random and meaningless.

prived of their regular browbeating, they turned out to be just like Americans.

There is plenty left, as there is after most revolutions: ethnics with a cultural grub stake, persons of an ecclesiastical temperament (the Church was once proud of not relying on these), and the quintessential Catholics who glory in being unfashionable. So too, England after the Reformation. The next generation will be the test. Meanwhile, the Right clings grimly to driftwood from the old Church and even hopes to put it together again, a possible new heresy in the making if the new Church tells them not to (see Brian Moore's excellent novella *Catholics*[2] in which a young inquisitor is sent from Rome to shut down the Latin mass in a corner of Ireland). And the radicals wade out bravely for unseen shores, defining themselves by action—fine while the action lasts: after Vietnam, we shall see.

One would expect from such a cataclysm a bristling literature of witness, with survivors rushing conflicting versions into print. But after the first burst, by ex-priests lashing at their past lives with the dull intolerance of outsiders—humility and arrogance snarled like steel wool in their prose—matters seem to have slowed to a trickle of bitter or facetious memoirs about addled sex instruction for boys and ridiculous sex instruction for girls. For instance, *Aphrodite in Mid-Century* by Caryl Rivers[3] emphasizes that the

[2]Brian Moore, *Catholics,* Holt, Rinehart & Winston.

[3]Caryl Rivers, *Aphrodite in Mid-Century: Growing up Female and Catholic in Postwar America,* Doubleday.

Church did not prepare one for Mickey Spillane: Miss
Rivers approaches this author as it were Voltaire, a
yawning trap for the faithful—but of course, it's all a
joke. In the case of John R. Powers' *The Last Catholic
in America*,[4] the gag is a book called *Sandra the Sex
Kitten, Hot from Cincinnati,* which young Powers an-
gled laboriously to obtain from the local drugstore in
the manner of a wheezing Woody Allen. For this one
needed a Church?

The accuracy of these and similar versions is not in
question—scores of parochial school victims can con-
firm them. What is surprising, coming from the
Whore of Rome, is their thinness. Rivers and Powers
write with the resolute brightness of Hollywood or
Catholic Digest clergy—or of such real-life celibates
as like to be up and doing. By contrast, Alexander
Portnoy has a sonorous intensity; and the mastur-
bating Irish hero of John McGahern's *The Dark* has
real tragic force.

The prepubescent jollity of so many American
Catholics says something about their obsessions. The
problem was sex and the solution was to remain too
young for it (viz., the faces of so many elder clergy). A
neutral reader confronted with such panicky stratagems might conclude that this was a singularly god-
less (to borrow its own phrase about communism) or
nontheocentric religion in its last days. Sex was at
the center, with everyone fleeing outward. The particular contract between God and man that had made
this Church either one of man's screwier pretensions
or else, Pascal's long shot, the actual incarnation of

[4]John R. Powers, *The Last Catholic in America,* Saturday Review Press.

God's Word—in any event a gaudy thing to have around—had been lost under a slag heap of forbidden movies and atrocious advice about masturbation; it may be written that the rock of ages devoted its last years to keeping its skirts down.

Certainly sex was never the battleground the professional theologians would have chosen. The New Testament is strikingly unsexy, for a religious source, and the fights that fashioned the early Church were over the nature of God, not the availability of condoms in Connecticut. So the Church's best and brightest weren't even interested in the only question much of the faithful wanted to hear about. The theologians were off talking of other matters when the roof fell in.

Birth control, a subject of virtually no theological interest, was the agent. Aesthetically it was right that a church that made such extravagant claims should gamble everything on a hopelessly unpopular position: this was precisely the supernatural element, the funky audacity Protestantism lacked. But in this case, the Church's mind wasn't even on the subject; the best theologians, like Hans Küng and Karl Rahner and Edward Schillebeeckx, who glittered in the conciliar period, were bored or embarrassed by it. (One of these, whom I knew personally, actually blushed and changed the subject when I brought up the Natural Law argument on birth control.) And one had the sickly suspicion that the official Church was simply saving face, à la Vietnam. The Church of England had reversed itself on birth control: but then smaller powers can give up their colonies and feel all

113

the better for it. "Birth control is not the point," the dying theologian cried. But it was the point, because sex had long since become more interesting than God, at least to parochial school victims (i.e., just about everybody).

About time, a secular reader might suppose. St. Paul's central proposition, that he had seen something more interesting than sex, was bound to wear thin after 2,000 years of second-hand repetition. Still, there was much specifically religious experience to be had right to the end, and its sudden disappearance, as if it had never been there, may have social consequences that haven't been examined yet. One obvious one is that it has left many Catholics with a hole in their personalities that they are trying frenziedly to fill (note the manic activity of ex-Catholics in so many fields from the peace movement to sex itself). It has unleashed a group of people with the highest metaphysical expectations, people bored and frustrated with lesser utopias or even ordinary human happiness. We were promised the sight of God face to face, and now you say it's a metaphor but come to church anyway.

Well, to hell with that. We laughed at the Protestants for that very thing, the noxious quality of religiousness for its own sake, symbolized by the gray suit and the apologetic manner. (And the more you reduce religious content, the more this quality obtrudes.) We, contrariwise, were raised on extremes, real flesh in the host and a real God in heaven; we had beliefs and not opinions. People might laugh at parsons, but they *hated* priests. Great! Protestants were respectable and sensible: we were outrageous, sons of the scarlet women. (Catholics of this persuasion agonized more over their own bourgeoisification than over any outside danger.) Bear in mind also that we were chronically overtrained for the little we were asked to do—after strict chastity and fasting worthy of guerrilla warriors, we were told to be good examples—and we brought much animal exuberance to the simple fact of being Catholic. This is an element I find missing in post-Vatican ruminations, which tend to be hangdog: one would expect even a false religious experience to have more balls than that.

One reason we may never get this historically valuable testimony is that American Catholics have more than usual difficulty with the first person, using it flippantly or defiantly or not at all. Humility was dumped over us like water on a hysteric, leaving us soggy and irritable, or passive, as the case might be. The sense of the word humility was that, although you were infinitely valuable in the eye of God, this was more to His credit than yours: it proved one more time that He could do anything, and your greatest value might be as a witness to that.

This feeling still makes Catholics uneasy with the school of religious autobiography, religion *as* autobiography, as recently promulgated by Harvey Cox. *Seduction of the Spirit*[5] is the ultimate in private judgment or black Protestant pride. A Coxite samples all the religion going until his palate is finely tuned

[5]Harvey Cox, *The Seduction of the Spirit: The Use and Misuse of People's Religion*, Simon & Schuster.

enough to know a vintage encounter group from a presumptuous High Mass. The book has been derisively called "Playboy's Guide to Religion in the Seventies," yet I believe Cox would half-seriously defend this title: why shouldn't the sensuous man add religion to his repertoire?

Catholics might agree to the theoretical worth of such writing, but it has always seemed flashy in the particular, unless the author heavily stressed his passivity to the will of God. And even this was usually best left to converts. Born Catholics wrote their confessional books on the way out, a last finger-wave at humility, and usually very messy (lack of practice, no doubt).

Thus Garry Wills' *Bare Ruined Choirs*,[6] which starts out to be definitive and then changes its mind, edges steadily away from the personal. Wills growing up Catholic is "we"; Wills grown up talks about "they"—liberal Catholics for the most part—and modestly disappears altogether. Well, since we *were* "we" to some extent and Wills describes that "we" beautifully, there's no point complaining about the missing self. But for the purposes of religious rhetoric (and most of Wills' book is written in rhetoric) a "they" requires an "I": as in, who's calling whom a heretic?

Wills clearly has it in for the liberal Catholics, and seems to accuse them of baring and ruining the choirs: but who are they in relation to him? Is he giving us liberal experience from the inside or the

[6]Garry Wills, *Bare Ruined Choirs: Doubt, Prophecy, and Radical Religion*, Doubleday.

outside? In either event, which liberal experience? Although I recognized an eye here and a nose there, I couldn't find a whole liberal I'd ever met. And small wonder, because Wills' model contains two trend-setting magazines, *Jubilee* and *Commonweal*,[7] that were barely on speaking terms, plus geographical zones of wildly different style, plus town and country, academy and soup kitchen, trendy Jesuit and moss-backed Benedictine.

These pheonomena can look like the same thing only from a great distance or a special perspective. And Wills' coyness about where he himself was sitting at the time amounts to a serious withholding of evidence. As a right-wing Thomist at a Jesuit seminary he could actually see all his enemies ranged along a single line, the way the *National Review* used to. The apolitical arties at *Jubilee* and the unaesthetic politicos at *Commonweal* could be sighted down the same barrel, and even Maisie Ward's (my mother's) "didactic publishing house"—which was almost entirely my father's (this last to get mother figures into his sights: mother figures must look truly menacing from seminaries).

To the trained eye, Wills' scattershot use of the concept "liberal" does in fact serve to place him well out-

[7] I had the rare experience of working for both of these. *Jubilee* was a spin-off of the Thomas Merton group at Columbia and its aim was largely aesthetic: to smarten up the taste of American Catholics. Naturally, it was snobbish. Politics was a dirty word there and mysticism ran way ahead of theology. At *Commonweal*, we breathed politics and theology, and none of the editors while I was there had any special artistic interests. In texture, dialogue, haberdashery, the magazines were two different worlds. Yet the word "liberal" was slapped on both, even as the *Daily News*' "pinko" stretched from Dean Acheson to Pablo Picasso.

side the fog (which may have a shape from outside) called liberalism. It was one of the ironies of American discourse in the Fifties that conservatives were always referring to "so-called liberals," but that they themselves did most of the so-calling. Liberals didn't usually think of themselves as liberals (unless they were debating Bill Buckley), but as this-ites or that-ites or just as sensible-ists; that is, they felt they were dealing with discrete issues discretely, and not as dependent parts of a fixed system. This in a sense was what *made* them liberals,[8] but the definition does not get us very far. There are thousands of ways of being unsystematic. In a Catholic setting, one might believe in the English mass, be open about situation ethics (a nominalist code which treats each case as potentially unique), but want no part of the Death of God. The very variety made you a liberal—but this tells us nothing about the subjects themselves, of the quality of the arguments or the arguers you were swayed by, all of which sound equally modish and superficial in *Bare Ruined Choirs*. Similarly, if you were a magazine carrying, as *Commonweal* did, punctiliously balanced articles on both sides of these questions, you were again a liberal just for adding to the modern Babel.

But if by liberal one simply means this, a sower of confusion, Garry Wills himself qualifies eminently. No liberal ever made the old Church sound quainter or more unworkable. And in the end, he seems to hold

[8] I recall an exotic conservative of the period (a Habsburg restorationist no less) asking a roomful of liberals what their "vision" was. They were nonplussed; he was triumphant. *You see? No vision.*

out hopes for the radical witness of the Berrigans—just the kind of authentic-sounding panacea liberals went for every time. If by liberal one means simply a holder of one or more new ideas, the term is too unwieldy and riddled with exceptions to be of any use at all.

I sense that Wills' use of the word is largely aesthetic anyway: signifying a natural distaste for the pointy-headed social engineer who (to take a secular parallel) believes in busing this year and community control the next, meanwhile irreparably damaging the organism that's already there. So too, the Catholic liberal empties the church with an English mass, then holds a symposium about bringing back Latin. Clearly it doesn't pay to make a mistake around Wills. Even though he admits that the old organism was in a desperately bad way, it seems it was the doctors that finally killed it. Otherwise, it might have lived another five minutes.

The aesthetic liberal is not really a satisfactory conception either. Like a *National Review*'s "typical left-wing intellectual," he sounds more like a faculty wife or a phys. ed. major grappling grimly with last year's ideas. The liberals (or nonconservatives) of the Fifties were accustomed to this line of heckling even then and the more intelligent of them learned from it, so that the Willses and Buckleys were constantly flogging the lame and the halt—e.g., Eleanor Roosevelt (great woman though she was) and Jacqueline Grennan, who brought up the rear. But Wills is not only unfair to whatever he means by liberal experience, he also withholds what he *does* know from within: the

119

*anti*liberal experience. Or, finally, the experience of his own conversion, if so there be, from conservatism to wherever he stands now. Just a few years ago, he was writing in a hearty Chestertonian manner that the trouble with Catholics was that they thought too much about being Catholic. Yet here he has gone and written a book on the subject himself, and what would his old self make of that?

Wills might very well answer that what he was doing and thinking was not that important, and that his subject is much larger than himself. This at least would be a suitably Catholic answer. For although Christians derive a tradition from Paul and Augustine of beginning the sermon with a confession or testimony—this is where I stand—Catholics have tended to abandon this to Protestants (everyone knows where Catholics stand), talking instead from some unstated magisterium about large matters and nothing but large matters. Wills would not dream of doing this in his fine political writings, but he is speaking here out of an older habit.

This habit tells us something about why ex-priests make such disappointing witnesses to their own history—they were too busy preaching to notice much of anything. To stray from Wills a moment: another dimly considered social consequence of Rome's troubles is the sudden emergence of all these trained preachers in the secular market; and not just any old preachers, but divinely ordained transmitters of infallible truth. Many priests and long-term seminarians carry the phantom magisterium with them into *every* field, even after leaving the Church, changing sides without dropping a stitch in their sermons or an ounce of their righteousness.

The habit is hard to shake, and I have heard newly married priests explaining the glories of their new state to battle-scarred laymen as if marriage had just been invented. And, of course, they mastered the theology of peace even more swiftly than Daniel Ellsberg. When the bright ones do it, the results can be exhilarating—scholastic thought or Teresan spirituality brought full blast to the secular—and a pleasant change from the ego-soaked exchanges we're used to. But the fact remains that the magisterium is imaginary now.[9] We *don't* know where Catholics stand, let alone ex-Catholics. And when Wills writes about the Church, his serene flow of Delphic assertions is not enough: we have to know that he himself was one of the alternatives liberals steered by.

Examples could be multiplied of Catholics shrinking from personal witness even where their witness is part of the necessary data. In Michael Novak's book *The Rise of the Unmeltable Ethnics*,[10] he registers a hot but disembodied indignation (something he calls "cultural rage," not a phrase you'd use if you were really angry) over the bigotry suffered by Slavs in western Pennsylvania, omitting to mention that he spent many of his formative years in a junior seminary where presumably Slavs were safe. Again it

[9]In Daniel Berrigan's recent admonition to the Israelis, he seemed to want them to be victims or Christ-figures indefinitely. But neither they nor many new revised Christians share the assumption that this is a good thing.

[10]Michael Novak, *The Rise of the Unmeltable Ethnics: Politics and Culture in the Seventies,* Macmillan.

THREE MOBS: LABOR, CHURCH AND MAFIA

looks like dishonesty, but isn't necessarily.

The town Novak was born in, Johnstown, Pa., was, I'm told, actually *worse* than he describes, and one year there could make a Slav feel like a nigger for life. Did Novak enter the seminary to get away from this? If so, it would tell us something about Ethnic Catholicism and its future. And if he told further of his personal rise, as a Slovak boy,[11] to the top of the ecumenical tree, feted by Wasp churchmen, it would tell us more. But, like many a busy theologian, he spurns the specific and escapes into generalization which, however ardently presented, lacks the force of a single fact.

At that, Novak is closer to the secular mainstream than most of his colleagues. There is plenty of "I feel" about Novak's writing, just not very much "I saw," and this tells more about Catholic style than most conscious accounts of it do. Abstract theology still smothered the Church when Novak and I were boys, and no human fact was big enough for us. The return to Biblical Christianity, and to the particular Catholic emphasis that "something happened"—not myth or stylized wonder story, but real history—came later. However much we welcomed it, we still tended to go

[11] In my original essay, I referred to Mr. Novak as Polish, and he wrote in to correct this foolish mistake. He went on to describe his early childhood as an earthly paradise—until, that is, he first encountered bigotry in a Catholic seminary. If so, I'm surprised he didn't make his book an attack on seminaries, rather than on Wasps and such. But Novak these days comes on as such a stage-ethnic, rolling his eyes and baring his teeth, and proving he can-so get really angry, that I don't know what to make of his testimony. His letter does not, for instance, point out any important distinction between Polish and Slovak experience in Western Pennsylvania; failing which, I must assume that they both came under the degrading rubric "honky," and that my original evidence from that area holds up.

on (as I am here), omitting proper nouns and writing nothing that couldn't be translated into Latin.

There again Wills is the best, and hence the best example, of his generation. He has a particular gift for writing abstractly for the Romans, while naming names for the heathen. His fine book *Nixon Agonistes* was actually about the end of Calvinism, but with enough good reporting (Nixon crouched in the shadows of his plane—Calvinism at bay) to make it seem like a personal portrait. His journalistic apostolate can produce misleading effects, when scholasticism is set too stridently to jazz. For instance, the garish chapter headings in *Bare Ruined Choirs,* "The Two Johns" (Kennedy and Roncalli) and "The Two Jackies" (Kennedy and Grennan), suggest that names not only make news, they also make theology. But the ensuing text actually comes closer to making fun of this widespread belief. Vatican II was probably called by John to forestall a vast schism, which was being prepared in a thousand places from Amsterdam to Tubingen. He wasn't opening any new windows; those had already been blown out one by one. He was accommodating to the wind. Or, as Tocqueville would say, a revolution only ratifies what has already happened.

Wills knows this almost too well. His catchy two Johns title conceals the fact that he isn't writing about either of them, but about the pair of them as liberal trends (the elastic in the word just fitting around both). JFK was *in effect* not crucially different from LBJ, it turns out, nor was John from Paul VI. "I live, not I, but liberalism lives in me." People are barely appearances behind which great ideas grapple; Nixon and Kennedy are funny faces worn by history and discarded.

There was that much platonism in every Catholic's milk, and conservatives had a double dose of it, believing in the style of Pius IX that liberalism "caused" things as opposed to things causing liberalism.[12] Applied to Vatican II, American Catholic platonism has a special remoteness: because analyzing the Council from an American point of view is like examining the causes of World War I from Australia. Wills tortuously compares Vatican II with the Vietnam war as liberal disillusionments. But Vatican II was not caused or shaped by American liberals, but by Europeans—different people on a different time scale, in no way comparable to JFK's pack of adventurers. European theology had been a scene of bloody trench warfare at least from the time of the Modernist crisis early in the century, which Wills, surprisingly provincial, whisks through at tabloid speed. When Hans Küng came here in the 1960s to bring Americans up to date on all this, he was shocked at how glibly we'd caught up. "It took us fifty years to get where we are, and you accept it immediately." I assume Wills knows all this and was happy to chase butterflies and hobby horses through various pages.

[12]If our definition of this word has been vague so far, observe the nineteenth-century Roman use of it. In the famous "Syllabus of Errors," liberalism covers pretty much the whole of secular thought and practice, including democracy itself. This was ideologism run riot. To the Romanist mind, the Enlightenment "caused" the French Revolution, liberalism "caused" the modern industrial state, and so on. That industrialism might equally have caused liberalism was an affront to the primacy of the Soul, and a hard pill for even contemporary Catholics to swallow.

America had little effect on the Council—our bishops hardly seemed to know what town they were in—except in matters of Church and state separation, where Americans could bring definite news from the future. But the Council[13] had devastating effects on Fortress America, and not just by nibbling away at the 50,000 readers of *Commonweal.* No doubt the liberal Fifth Column had something to do with these devastating effects. But in retrospect, the only thing that could have prevented them was to keep out Europe altogether, not to mention our own friendly Protestant theologians. The hatches could hardly have been tighter in any case. French Dominicans had a devil of a time getting *imprimaturs* over here; *Commonweal* was banned in the diocese of Los Angeles. The hysterical repression, symbolized as farce by Cardinal Spellman's slashing forays at *Baby Doll* and *The Moon Is Blue,* had to burst open. The question was when and how.

The first thing to understand about the Catholic religion is its cultish nature. Non-Catholics were always asking, how can you possibly believe this far-out doctrine or that, and much labor went into the finding of ingenious answers. But not one Catholic that I knew stayed in the Church because of these answers. We stayed because of the sacraments, i.e., actual physical exchanges through mouth, ear, touch with the Godhead, and because of a promise of brotherhood through this. The Church was a constellation of practices, built around specific holy places, but also

[13]By Council I mean the whole continuum of change; the Council itself had a surprisingly conservative place in this continuum.

around a movable temple, and this seemed to meet the paired psychic needs for permanence and change, dignity and recklessness.

The Gospels suggest that God can tear down every one of his temples and scatter his people; yet also that it is good to rebuild the temple. The roster of saints includes abbots and men in rags jeering at abbots, and we were taught improbably to learn something from both: the dispossessed holy man, constantly moving and making a living church out of people, and the keeper of the shrine after he has passed on. Around these shrines there gradually grew a culture, absorbing the local atmosphere and including the previous culture, which in sum was both the Church's glory and a potential object of the next holy man's wrath.

When applied to this country, this old-world dialectic presented certain difficulties. European Catholicism, as it was, was never a comfortable culture for a young country on the make. New England Congregationalism and its variants suited the landscape perfectly, with the bright blank white chapel as our fixed holy place. Compare the uncertainties of Catholic Church architecture, from pseudo-European to furtive Yankee. And, for holy men, America had its bands of revivalists, tent singers, testifiers, the gaudiest crop of spiritual entertainers ever seen. Compare the immigrant Catholic preacher, who could bring no eye-boggling word from the religious frontier, telling of gold strikes and the future, but could only instruct his flock to remember certain things from the past.

Even the heresies didn't match. For native Americans, Pelagianism was the one, the belief that man can do it all, with or without divine grace. (A strange reading of Calvinism to be sure, but the pioneers were not theologians and they got what they wanted from religion: adrenaline and the Coach's silent approval.) From Catholic Europe another heresy was imported, consisting of various degrees of *de facto* quietism. Let God's will be done. Render unto Caesar. Holy obedience (a curious distortion). Know thy place. It was a heresy that didn't even suit the huddled immigrants for very long, with their new prospects, but it was urged on them anyway for generations and was part of the breaking point later.

John Cogley's *Catholic America*[14] is a splendidly concise account of the groping of Catholics for a cultural soil, and I recommend it for its almost eerie balance. Cogley used to be a titan among Catholic underachievers. At *Commonweal* he was our sage, an intuitive and unstuffy moralist full of restless good sense. Yet in secular surroundings there was always a sense of stiffness and of best-Sunday-suit about him. Hence his book is a detached source book rather than the full-blooded statement one had hoped for. Typically he describes *Commonweal* and the *Catholic Worker* without revealing his own deep involvement in both: hence, no color, no poetry. No ego.[15]

[14]John Cogley, *Catholic America*, Dial.

[15]Since writing the above, I learn that Cogley has jumped to Lambeth. His reasons are quite logical—he prefers the doctrines over there—yet again he may underestimate the poetic and cultish associations of religion which make such comparison-shopping psychologically difficult, as Jews who christianize have discovered. These are the associations I miss in his book.

THREE MOBS: LABOR, CHURCH AND MAFIA

Brooding over Cogley's findings, I am more and more convinced (perhaps of the obvious) that the immigrants' difficulties with English played a cruel part in delaying the alternate American proposition they might have made. Even many Irishmen were relatively new to the language (O'Connell's assault on Gaelic came only a decade before the Famine), and Catholic schools promptly perpetuated a pathetically bad English prose in which it is difficult to think at all. I was reminded of this prose by certain young Watergate witnesses.

A comical game commenced in which new Catholics tried to plant an American style of Catholic culture while rejecting the ground on which it could grow, i.e., the secular culture around it. The phrase un-American was turned wantonly against those most at home here. Eleanor Roosevelt, for instance, was a bad American mother. A skeptical old Yankee like Oliver Wendell Holmes was a very dubious American. And so forth. It was pure negation, just as anticommunism was pure negation, because the Church had no serious alternative culture that really looked American, outside of some very American quirks like St. Christopher medals on cars and Bing Crosby, more a hobby than a culture.

Thus the Church could not propose itself, except in the vaguest terms. It could only counter communism with a "return to God" (what God?) and with "spiritual values" (whatever they were). It could denounce bad Americans and praise neutral ones (mostly J. Edgar Hoover) who lacked the bad ones' qualities. But it could not point to another *kind* of good Ameri-

can, outside of pure symbols like Knute Rockne or
Father Duffy, because there was no content. The
bishops were glorified messenger boys from Rome,
and they couldn't do much with the Syllabus of Errors
or half the curial output.

Americans can't think like Italian cardinals (few
people can), but this group couldn't even think
against them, like the French or Dutch: because they
had been endowed with half-baked Latinate minds
with no specific national strengths or stratagems. As
for their flocks, these had to be obedient in a vacuum,
receiving no instructions worth hearing about life on
this continent. Neither leaders nor led could make a
culture of this, only an amalgam of quaintnesses plus
an awful lot of football. (In the colonial situation,
what passes for style may simply be the awkwardness
of the natives at coping with the imperial customs—
like a Bushman in a dinner jacket.) The liberals had
to look silly with their clumsily worn European styles
and their dabbling in the Mexican and Creole; but it
would have been just as phony to join the Holy Name
or root for Immaculate Conception High. For more
substance, the American Church had to look to Europe; and when Europe gave back the wrong signals,
the American Church was finished. Because it had
nothing to turn to inside itself.

Or at least the fixed temple was finished and the
flock was dispersed: time no doubt for the wandering
holy men, the Berrigans, and we'll see what else. But
more seriously, the brotherhood was broken. It used
to be a pious commonplace to say that one would
remain a Catholic if one were the last one on earth.

But it doesn't work that way. The set of beliefs might remain intact, but the cult would be gone. The mass is a communal feast, and one cannot dine alone. Many people left the Church because other people were leaving, not so flabby a reason as it seems. We had a pact with each other to believe and to sustain each other in belief; and I sense this pact perversely intact among ex-Catholics. If you don't believe, then I don't either.

But the problem is not so much one of personal belief (which for most Catholics grew out of a way of life, an effect as much as a cause), but of building and sustaining cultures of any kind in the modern world. The intellectual side of things hasn't changed that much since Tertullian's *"credo quia impossibile."* We always knew the doctrines were far-fetched. And the arguments that ex-Catholics bring against the Church (as in Michael Harrington's *Fragments of the Century,* a showcase of impersonal autobiography— even ex-Catholics can be hag-ridden by humility[16]) were making the rounds in Ivan Karamazov's day. The difference is that until recently only men of Harrington's scrupulous intellectual conscience gave these arguments commanding weight.

Against them Catholics offered a living culture and the sacramental experience. Of course, there were rational arguments too, because it was heresy for a Universal Church to neglect the mind; but the exis-

---

[16]Michael Harrington, *Fragments of the Century,* Saturday Review Press. *Fragments of the Century* is only partly about religion, and therefore out of bounds for this essay. In passing, I would say it makes the case for its method: the author is a historical object, sometimes witness, sometimes victim, occasionally initiator. Who can say more?

tence of an Index of Forbidden Books implied that most people aren't very good at thinking, either them or us, and if one argued to a tie with the heathen, that was fair enough. (Thomistic phraseology guaranteed at least a tie, on account of darkness.) At any rate thinking was optional, and we answered the Harringtons mostly with the simple fact of Catholicism itself: the liturgical cycle, Advent, Lent, a life within a life that seemed to work whatever its theoretical underpinnings.

Whether this life can go on, without a culture, in strictly movable temples, is the next question. European Catholics could drop dogma and still remain Catholic: leaving the Church was a fundamental act, like changing your name, as opposed to an incidental, like changing your mind. But here the associations are thinner. The only authentic Catholic culture was in the immigrant cities, and as people began to leave these, their affirmations became strident and their religion jerry-built. The Catholicism of the postwar suburbs was as ersatz as the super-Americanism of the Fifties: something that no longer came naturally and must therefore be mimed ostentatiously. High time for death by television and the present, in which Church business is falling off roughly as much as movie business or any other business that can't be done from your car. Culture has long since given way to fashion as it has in the arts and elsewhere, and religion has entered a cycle of little fake deaths and rebirths like the rise and fall of the hemline.

If a new culture is now impossible, and the old one can only be restored by cosmetics, religion will have to make do with fashion as a base—quite a challenge to the Holy Spirit. Harvey Cox's religious smorgasbord, with the customer darting from plate to plate consuming all the religious experience he can swallow, is one style; Andrew Greeley's trust in archetypal religious symbols is another—though whether these symbols are all that archetypal when stripped of their cultural wrappings has yet to be proved. (Father Greeley's *New Agenda* is an awesome example of clerical optimism, i.e., of surveying the current scene and deciding it's exactly what we wanted. He might be right—but I'd like to know what situation he would *not* find a wonderful challenge and chance to grow.) An amusing cat-chasing-its-tail game to watch is the hip clergyman making the Church sensible for today's young moderns only to find that they want it wild and mystical, at which point he gives them witchcraft, at which point ... never suspecting that it's *him* they're avoiding. And look for the carnival to roll on of Jesus freaks and holy fools and other illuminati, fulfilling at least religion's primal duty to be entertaining.

Meanwhile the old Church looks on, waiting to see what it has to work with, still convinced of its survival powers, if of little else, and ready to pounce. Much has been made of the Church's fondness for right-wing climates, and no doubt the books that come out every year exposing clerical corruption are all too true. But the quintessential Church simply wants, like ITT, a safe place to set up its curious shop, dispensing sacraments and spreading the Word. Right now I would say that the communist countries present a far more suitable ground for the Church's work than America ever did—but that's another subject.

The one kind of society that the Church cannot adjust to is no society at all, i.e., a setup where community has become so fragmented that a communal religion is a fiction, sustained only by talk and make-news items in the press and television. A religion is simply a society in one of its aspects; and if the American Catholic Church is scattered and confused right now (and even its best friends don't deny it), consider the rest of America. The cure, if it comes, would include a cultural revolution affecting many things besides the Catholic Church.

III

Everybody's Mafia

As with God in the late Middle Ages, all that there is to know about the Mafia seems to be known by now except whether it actually exists. Among recent exegetes, Professor Joseph Albini[1] finds the evidence so conflicting that no single Mafia can be deduced. Like a street-corner rationalist looking for contradictions in the Bible, Albini believes that when two accounts differ they must both be wrong, and that separate names (Cosa Nostra, the Outfit, etc.) must necessarily stand for different things.

Nicholas Gage[2] finds the fragmented testimony of such canaries as Valachi and Nicola Gentile sufficient to prove the opposite—with a secret society bound to silence, it's about all the evidence you're going to get. Gay Talese,[3] who writes like a man on a tapped phone with a gun in his ear, suggests that there may indeed

[1]Joseph L. Albini, *The American Mafia: Genesis of a Legend*, Appleton-Century-Crofts.

[2]Nicholas Gage, *The Mafia Is Not an Equal Opportunity Employer*, McGraw-Hill.

[3]Gay Talese, *Honor Thy Father: The Inside Book on the Mafia*, World.

135

be such a thing but that the American branch consists by now of tired businessmen on the way down. Mario Puzo,[4] as a novelist, has no professional opinion to offer, but knows a good myth when he sees one.

Puzo at least is right. The ineffable Norman Podhoretz recently ascribed our interest in gangsters to our need for success stories (given time, Podhoretz would undoubtedly find sublimated success drives in *Love Story* and *The Sound of Music*). But surely no explanation is necessary. The myth of feudal bandits dumped down on twentieth-century Brooklyn is so intrinsically fascinating that even the characters in the real thing, who ought to know better, are tempted to believe it, making it a fact in its own right.

For instance, several gangsters have congratulated Mr. Puzo on his uncanny portrayal of their profession in *The Godfather,* even though Puzo confesses (in *The Godfather Papers*)[5] that he had never met a gangster in his life. Which means either that the Corleones are just a typical Sicilian family, or—somewhat more likely—that if you make a portrait brave and noble enough, people will see themselves in it somehow.

Similarly, much has been made by unbelievers of the fact that mafiosi never use the word Mafia. But in recent testimony in Boston, Joe "Barbosa" Baron did indeed use it, doubtless having picked it up in his reading. Hoods are as suggestible as the next fellow, and an old friend of Joey Gallo says that Crazy Joe used to think he was Richard Widmark before he had

[4]Mario Puzo, *The Godfather,* Putnam's.

[5]*The Godfather Papers and Other Confessions,* Putnam's.

models closer to home. So we may get a Mafia yet, if those lines around *The Godfather* movie pay attention.

To judge from Albini's book (which, allowing for special pleading excessive even in a scholar protecting his turf, seems to be a reasonably thorough historical study), the Mafia has always been a myth, but in this same potent sense of a religious myth, like a nonexistent saint who works real miracles. Mafia legends may be sturdier than the real thing. It is, in fact, virtually impossible to trace what became of the real thing between its alleged founding in 1282 and its re-emergence in 1860: indeed, even the founding is in doubt. The phrase "*Morte Alla Francia Italia Anela,*" which Gage blithely passes on as the origin of the term, could not have been used at that time because Sicily did not consider itself part of Italy (Albini, as usual, beats you to death with other reasons, but this one should do). But the basic legend of a local girl being avenged against a French officer provided a symbol with or without the slogan, a Garden of Eden, worthy of a man of respect.

The subsequent history of the Mafia suggests a series of *ad hoc* brotherhoods that folk history has somehow run together. For some thousand years, anyone who could rent a boat could occupy Sicily, and the natives found it necessary to improvise outlaw structures to cope with each occupation in turn. Obviously a myth of unbroken resistance could be used to lend legitimacy and authority to such kangaroo governments, and it seems likely that some groups claimed more history than they were strictly entitled to: for instance, the Beati Paoli, who believed they were descended from the Minor Brethren of St. Francis and still had powers of priesthood conferred in 1185. A secret society can always surface under new management and claim it was there all along—as to some extent the IRA has done in our own time. In Sicily, as in Ireland, the shortage of official history gave the field to unofficial history, and the cult of a 700-year-old Mafia has endured as an inspiration and occasional embarrassment to the present members.

Thus, anyway, Professor Albini. And since the links are undoubtedly missing, the historic Mafia may be called for now a functioning superstition. Gage and Talese both leap gracefully over some 600 years of Mafia evolution, allowing only that it seems to have changed sharply by the nineteenth century. Looking at our present version, one notes among American Mafia families little sign of the mystic continuity necessary for such long life. In *Honor Thy Father,* the Bonanno gang begins to split the moment Joe appoints his son Bill to the succession. Far from honoring such blood loyalty, the lower ranks mumbled about nepotism just like regular executives and jumped to other organizations for upward mobility. Even in *The Godfather,* which seems to exalt family ties beyond anything in actual experience, a rival gang leader takes it for granted that he can do business with the son if he can manage to kill the father first. The fact that he can't may be why, in Oscar Wilde's phrase, we call it fiction.

The gap between Mafia legend and fact is what makes the mafiosi so richly and, for them, inconveniently dramatic, whether for comedy or tragedy. There are certainly plenty of other gangsters, Jewish and Irish and whatnot. But how many of them believe they are blood descendants of a great patriotic movement? The stately sense of honor and loyalty makes even their silence dramatic. Nobody ever invoked the Fifth with such panache. If I were Sicilian, I would think twice before disowning them completely, cant notwithstanding. When Lucky Luciano guaranteed the protection of the Florida coast in World War II, he was doing no more than Francis Drake would have done. If they receive undue attention, it is not just because of bigotry, but because they are men to whom attention must be paid, knight errants gone wrong and not to be mistaken for your usual pig thief.

Of course it's a myth. Out of the desperate history of Sicily, it would be too much to hope for such flowers. The style is miracle enough. If mafiosi really had the honor and loyalty they profess, they would not need to kill each other half so often. The famous Banana war,[6] like all the other Mafia wars, was no tale of heroic vengeance but a squalid exchange of double-cross and triple-cross worthy of a major world power. And in all these books, even Puzo's dithyramb, I found somewhat less loyalty and honor than in Albert Speer's memoirs. What they would behave like without their myth of nobility shakes the imagination.

Perhaps the Mafia has traveled badly and American air doesn't suit it. Young Bill Bonanno is as dis-

---

[6]Presumably so called because the name Bonanno captured the fancy of the New York *Daily News* headline writers.

mayed as his father before him by the decline in discipline among the younger hoods, although the more spectacular betrayals are still performed by the elders. But to judge from Barzini's notes on the subject,[7] or Albini's, Mafia honor at best was barely enough for thieves to get by on. The early brotherhoods were desperate amalgams which found robbing in packs more effective than robbing singly. The early appearance of blood oaths indicates how little spontaneous trust there ever was among them. One theory on the mainland was that they were really Arabs anyway, and perhaps there is an Arab touch to their individualism and paranoid gallantry; but mostly what they were was starving.

Anyway there is no occasion for funny blood theories. The Sicilians were as adaptable as anyone else would be whose history keeps coming unstuck. One colonization is bad enough; numerous ones splinter the personality to madness. The spiritual response, as in Ireland, was to give themselves more tradition than they needed. But the physical response was to cooperate with every invader who came along, from the Bourbons to Garibaldi to the American army in World War II. And even over here they are ultrapatriots to the legitimate non-Sicilian government. Far from being a national liberationist movement gone sour, the Mafia could almost be defined as those who sold out first and best, the supercolonials. And of course they sold out the only thing they had to sell, their own people. What they offered in each case was the same gimcrack feudalism, based on a patron-

[7] Luigi Barzini, *From Caesar to the Mafia,* Library Press.

client network, claiming all kinds of bloodlines but in fact being a shifting meritocracy of courage, shrewdness, and cruelty.

When they came to this country, the Sicilians found only one trifling difference in political organization from what they were used to. Instead of a new government arriving every few years, new subjects arrived, causing roughly the same net effect of institutional unraveling. Theoretical legitimacy might exist in Washington and in those remote backwaters known as state capitals, but actual social legitimacy had to be established over and over again with each new group. This was pre-eminently the land of the *ad hoc* brotherhood and the kangaroo court. From Grand Kleagle to baseball commissioner, private law always existed alongside public, and an immigrant could be pardoned for confusing the two.

In the cities where the Sicilians settled, the Irish had already established their own legitimacy. One way and another (history records no clean ones), they had captured the official titles and were the "law." But Sicilians were not fooled by this. The city machines were no more the law than the Bourbons had been. In fact, the Sicilian saw nothing much here to surprise him: patronage and pay-off, justice as political adjustment, cops as mercenaries, politics in the raw, too young to cover itself respectably. It is Albini's contention that the Mafia was imported solely as technique, but even this was hardly necessary, since everything but the language was already here, from Tammany down to the Irish betting parlors.

That, for Albini and to some extent Talese, is that.

THREE MOBS: LABOR, CHURCH AND MAFIA

Standard Mafia apologetics leans hard on this simi-
larity to other American institutions. Bill Bonanno,
through his mouthpiece Talese, broods at length over
the hypocrisies of private business and public justice.
What are we doing that's different? he says. (The per-
suasiveness of this defense depends partly on how you
feel about other American institutions.) Albini for his
part sees no need to conjure up an international con-
spiracy. Mafiosi tend to be intensely local. They haven't even infiltrated eastern Sicily, let alone the
Italian mainland (recent news reports say they have,
but every crime wave looks like Mafia to mainland-
ers). Wherever a local situation demands it, some
Sicilians will fall back on Mafia technique, forming
secret brotherhoods, enforcing their own laws (rather
heavy on capital punishment, but what can you do
when you haven't got prisons?), and making whatever
deals they can with the current Bourbons; even perhaps, pretending to a history, a continuity, that isn't
there.

In real life, according to Albini, the early American
Mafia did not even know it was a Mafia until it read
about itself in the papers: it was simply a blanket
phrase for a lot of disconnected local groups, some
relatively honest, applied indiscriminately by a sala-
cious press. As usual, Albini pushes his theory outra-
geously hard. For instance, in discussing the famous
Hennessy case, which seemed to locate a self-
conscious Mafia unit in New Orleans in 1890, he says
the murder of police superintendent Hennessy could
not have been a true Mafia job because the leader
paid the killers bonuses, and he wouldn't have had to

if he already had their sworn allegiance. If that
doesn't sound like a defense lawyer down to his last
trick, at least it doesn't sound like the voice of impar-
tial scholarship.

But so far the point may be largely academic
anyway. An international crime syndicate in the
1890s would have been a cumbersome affair at best.
The question is not whether the Mafia has a past but
whether it has a future. The standard post-Valachi
version, as repeated by Gage and others, is that the
new, revised Mafia only came into being in the 1930s,
after the night of the Sicilian Vespers, when Lucky
Luciano stepped over forty or thirty or ninety dead
bodies (accounts vary as much as Joe McCarthy's
lists) and began organizing the survivors into a
modern business. Albini rebuts this notion by
pointing out that nobody has ever named the actual
victims. This may not be conclusively important: to be
credited with a killing is almost as good as doing it, in
that world of rumor and bluff. What is important is
Albini's further claim that Luciano never organized
anything at all outside of New York, and even in the
city was no more than an arbitrator among families,
and a not very effective one at that.

This gets us at last to the nub of the matter. If Luciano did not organize the Mafia, did anybody else?
Or is it still just a series of shifting alliances with no
one mind of its own? Albini is at his most strenuous
in discrediting the evidence of a National Mafia
Commission, and he dismisses the convocation at
Apalachin on the following dubious grounds, among
others: observers got the numbers wrong again (but

it's hard to count men running through the bushes); crime syndicates have been known to meet before on an impromptu basis, which doesn't imply a permanent organization (but the other meeting he cites, in Atlantic City in 1929, did not consist entirely of Italian families); the representation does not square with our knowledge of Family power structure and therefore there is none, only a constant shift of power relations. (OK, our reading of that was too rigid. Our canaries only saw part of the forest.)

For his *coup de grâce,* Albini adds that the alleged commission was not able to prevent the Banana wars —which is rather less than proving that the United Nations doesn't exist because it never stopped anything. Obviously the commission is not so powerful that it can prevent a powerful family from defying it. But we do learn from Talese's book that members of the Bonanno family had trouble getting work during the wars and that many of them defected as a result. Which is a lot more than the UN can usually manage.

Similarly, in hacking away at the myth of an international Mafia, Albini sweats a little too hard for his own good. Reading him, you would suppose there were no contacts at all between American mafiosi and the old country. For instance, he nowhere mentions Vito Genovese's enforced sabbatical in Sicily, during which he was of such service to the U.S. Army and after which he did so much to get the Mafia into the narcotics trade. Nor does he go into Luciano's Old Boys convention in pre-Castro Cuba, which proved so embarrassing to Frank Sinatra. Since the drug business depends heavily on international cooperation between dishonest men, the vestigial blood loyalties of the Mafia might be expected to give them an edge here. But Albini's Mafia, being nonexistent, would not know what to do with an edge.

The myth of a monolithic international machine may be easy to dispose of, for now, on psychological grounds alone. The question is whether, in this age of mergers and lightning communication, the Mafia has resisted bigness altogether and remained uniquely a cottage industry. The quick answer, comforting mainly to Italians, is that if it has it will shortly be crowded out by more cosmopolitan syndicates. The word may survive even this, and is already used loosely to cover crime of all races, but it won't be the same.[8]

In fact, each of these books except Albini's conveys a certain nostalgia about the old Maf, an unusually nostalgic organization to begin with. Nowadays the Mob can barely find enough hungry Italian boys and so far refuses to replace them with lesser breeds—presumably because these would lack the necessary honor. When Joey Gallo was in prison, he toyed with the idea of giving black gunmen equal employment, but the results were not encouraging. Joe Colombo was killed by one, and who could have hired him but Joey?

[8]As Gage points out, the Mafia has always coexisted with local crime syndicates, such as the Purple Hand Gang in Detroit, the Cleveland Syndicate, etc. Since their work looks roughly the same, it is easy to confuse them and lump them under one heading. But an international syndicate would need to stitch together not only these organizations, for American distribution purposes, but also assorted Turkish politicians, French middlemen, Vietnamese talent scouts, and God knows what else. And who is better equipped to assemble such packages than the Mafia?

THREE MOBS: LABOR, CHURCH AND MAFIA

It is clearly in the Mafia's interest to appear to be going out of business, but to a flourish of trumpets, which these books provide. The Mafia soul has always been split between secrecy and ostentation. If the secret is too well kept, who will respect them? Gage describes the ornate interiors of their houses, compared with the drab front they must show the tax man. Talese contrariwise contrasts the meanness of their hide-outs and all-round dullness of their lives with the "compulsion to travel first-class on airplanes, to lease a Cadillac."

Both versions would seem to be correct. A *capo* who lives too well is in danger from his own people: several have been gunned down for their conspicuous consumption—living well is revenged the best. Meyer Lansky was safer in an anonymous Florida cottage than a don in a gilded fortress. On the other hand, a man must impress his clients somehow. So one arrives at these enormously complex façades: not just silk on the inside and cloth on the outside, but a constant switch back and forth depending on who's looking. Thus the mania for respectability: the plain gray suit and the flashing ring. In the circumstance it is quaint of Bill Bonanno to rail at the hypocrisy of more orthodox public figures.

Gay Talese has been criticized for writing what amounts to promotional material for the Bonanno family, but his book is an invaluable document and I don't know how such books can be obtained without some compromise. It is a lot to ask of an author that he betray the confidence of a Mafia family. As with a tapped phone call, one must interpret the message. *Honor Thy Father* conveys at least what the Bonannos would like you to think of them, or what they wouldn't mind you thinking of them. Talese signals occasionally to his educated audience—dull, aren't they? Almost pathetic. But that's all he can do. Our language differs from theirs about a few words like "dull." (God knows, they would find Sidney Hook's life dull.) But beyond that, Talese must play it straight.

His account of Bill Bonanno's thought processes is therefore all the more illuminating for being precisely the way Bill would like you to get it. When I add that it reminded me of Yogi Berra reading Gospel comics, this is not to indicate that Bill seems stupid. On the contrary. He is stupid only in the one area where he can't afford to be intelligent, that is, in questions of moral legitimacy. Here he becomes like a scientist hanging onto a fundamentalist religion. He argues like a well-drilled child, going over the same responses again and again, and never moving forward an inch. We're only doing what everybody else does, the Banana war is nothing compared with Vietnam (that mighty mother of excuses), we're only providing for needs that society is too hypocritical to recognize —fair enough if you include listening to the juke box and hauling grain among these. The Mafia uses legitimate businesses to "dry clean" its money—and apparently its members' consciences.[9]

---

[9]"By entering legitimate business they establish sources of income that appear legal and often pay just enough taxes to avoid prosecution. The legitimate businesses give them opportunities to reinvest money in the rackets. Such businesses themselves can be extremely profitable, especially when the Mob succeeds through terror tactics in gaining a local or regional monopoly"—Michael Dorman, *Payoff,* McKay. Dorman adds that Mafia campaign contributions look better when they come from "businessmen."

THREE MOBS: LABOR, CHURCH AND MAFIA

Thus the dramatic problem that *The Godfather* fails to resolve in either book or film and that makes it finally only superior melodrama turns out to be a pseudoproblem. How, we had wondered, could a nice boy like *The Godfather's* Michael Corleone become a ravening killer? Puzo makes up incidents galore and even takes us inside Michael's head, but the join is never satisfactory. We go from Jekyll to Hyde, with no believable chemical in between.

But Bill made the same transition in real life and we are also offered his head, or at least his words, to examine, and there's simply nothing there—just a few catechism answers he'd absorbed as a child in case they came in handy. Entering his father's business was no more of a moral crisis than joining the army and killing somebody there. If he had not been drafted he would have carried his bloody catechism unused to the grave, as a civilian carries his My Lai.[10]

Unfortunately the author cannot follow Bill all the way to the trenches. Talese's role was like that of a Mafia child, or, as Bill Bonanno might say, like a U.S. citizen under Johnson, assured that the other guy started it and that daddy detests violence. Talese's

[10]According to the Banana code, the Mafia will wither away the day that all human pleasures are declared legal. The American Mafia was originally conjured up simply to help move booze, stayed around to gamble, and creaked into the drug era, with some of the older *capos* protesting (they love children, it seems). The trouble with all this is that, even if there were no crimes left (and who can bet they wouldn't come up with a new one?), the Mafia's mode of operation would remain criminal almost by definition. As a large outlaw apparatus, it would still lack politicians and judges and have to buy a piece of someone else's; lack social sanction and have to improvise its own, etc. So that even if *all* its businesses were legitimate, it would be some distance from the respectability that Bill Bonanno craves.

account of the Banana war seems disingenuous even
on a reading of texts. Nicholas Gage states categori-
cally that Joe Bonanno had contracts out to kill the
archdukes of the Luchese and Gambino families and
that the contracts fell into the wrong hands—Joe Colombo's, as it happened—lighting the whole string of
crackers. Talese ascribes the contracts to a loyal but
muddled lieutenant of Bonanno's, acting for once in
his life without orders. (This lieutenant died shortly
afterward of heart failure, the Mafia's No. 1 killer.)
And during the war itself, according to Talese, we are
not to suppose young Bill did any actual killing. Some
days he went to work like a Jane Austen gentleman
who does something or other in the City; other days,
he hid out and worried about his weight, every fluc-
tuation of which is carefully recorded; but in neither
case was he anything but passive.

Some critics have found mischief in this apparent
whitewash, but the writer as Mafia child has an interesting vantage point. With the violence down to a
dull roar off stage, we get a better look at the way of
life all that blood[11] is paying for. There is a brooding
sense of self-pity and injured innocence in the Bonanno household that infects even their pleasures. Joe
Bonanno loves to read about himself but everybody
gets him wrong and he is in no position to correct

[11]In this case, Mafia blood. How well Bugsey Siegel's boast, or lament,
"we only kill each other," holds up generally is hard to say. Gage says that
Mafia loan sharks can be quite reasonable, even friendlier than Chase
Manhattan ones at times. But again, the Mob needs it both ways—a reputation for killing, a reputation for not killing—and our hard-breathing
law officers will have to solve a lot more murders before we know how
much of either is deserved.

149

them. Young Bill loves to travel first-class but dares not stick his head out the front door. Even when he goes to jail he cannot cash in on his small power. Candy bars are sneaked in to him, but he can't eat them in case they're poisoned. The grievance throbs like a nonstop migraine. If we're only doing what everybody does, why can't we enjoy it the way they do? Bill even lacks every American's birthright, a credit card, and is caught using someone else's: a fine ending for a man of respect.

Talese's book has a further peculiar advantage of a kind that can only happen once. The method he has chosen, that of the nonfiction novel or new journalism or whatever it's called this month, would be, at least as practiced here, an unfortunate strategy for most subjects. Talese uses the resources of fiction all right —but what fiction! For instance, to vivify scenes where he was not present himself, he decorates with things that are *likely* to have happened, those lifelike things we all do—i.e., Bill loosens his tie when he boards his plane, stretches his legs, etc.—little wax flowers of description that give off the same unreality as bad Victorian novels. But this proves to be weirdly right for the subject. The prose matches the stiff, watchful façade of the Mafia. One is reminded of a touched-up country wedding photo, with the cheeks identically rouged and the eyes glazed, of the kind the Bonanno family might have ordered for themselves back in Sicily.

Mario Puzo profits from the same oddity. He has said that he wishes he'd written *The Godfather* better —and he certainly could have, being not only a gifted writer but a knowing one. (Read *The Godfather Papers,* a first-rate collection of essays only glancingly related to *The Godfather,* hence outside our present scope.) But a better book might have been less true to the subject. The stilted, frequently abstract dialogue of hack fiction echoes precisely the ruminations of Bill Bonanno in real life. Mafiosi would seem to love the cosmic orotund phrase that good writers despair of finding and bad writers find all the time. Puzo may go too far in equipping his killers with quasi-artistic temperaments, but their response, again in real life, suggests that this is not displeasing to them.

Interestingly enough, this avowedly commercial novel has been transposed note for note into a film apparently acceptable to the high-brow—which may say something about why high-brows go to films and don't read novels. Of course, the book's in-between bits, the arbitrary jumps from head to head, the had-I-but-knowns ("if someone had told her she would not see Michael again until three years passed, she would not have been able to bear the anguish of it"), the speed-writing clichés ("his face red with fury," "the smiles vanished from the faces of . . ."), and the I-give-up transitions ("the change in him [Michael] was . . . extraordinary") have been dumped and replaced by specific movie virtues. Still one wonders if book-people haven't surrendered too much to film in drumming melodrama out of literature. In its very artificiality, melodrama offers specific literary possibilities lacking in naturalism. And our Puzos might be tempted to write those in-between bits better if such efforts were not foredoomed to be called commercial.

THREE MOBS: LABOR, CHURCH AND MAFIA

This is by the way. The novel remains at least an excellent screenplay and the movie is preposterously entertaining, telling Puzo's compendium of old time Mafia anecdotes with all the gravity of Old Testament epic. Marlon Brando as the Godfather does everything wrong, even his self-consciously Italian hand gestures are out of synch with his words, but in an atmosphere where solemn hamming is to the point, this doesn't matter as much as it might. Brando is in an unhappy phase of his career where he seems to be wondering, how can I be great in this role? and he interprets until the sweat runs.

But the rest of the cast conveys the precise guts of the Mafia myth, the engorged self-respect and self-importance, the theatrical secretiveness, the eerie sense of play, as though it were all really an opera after all. Al Pacino's face in frequent close-up does all that can be done for Michael's baffling motivation. (I didn't know a face could take that much close-up and still say anything.) James Caan as Sonny Corleone conveys the empty geniality that backs onto homicidal rage better than Widmark ever did. And Robert Duvall as the non-Italian *consigliere* has all the weasel cunning of the outsider signed on by the Myth but not really part of it.

There are some other things to praise in the movie —the interior sets, which convey everything that Gage and Talese have to say about Mafia home life, the stately operatic movement from tableau to tableau, and the extraordinarily clear articulation of the story line. As to the violence, I have to disqualify myself. I don't enjoy it and therefore don't look at it.

Like a surgeon I heard about who walked out of *M.A.S.H.*, I don't like to watch people suffer if I can't help them. I am told that the violence in *The Godfather* is quite elegant and suitably unreal. To hell with it.

In one sense Talese and Puzo would seem to cancel out in their moral effect—Talese demythologizing as fast as Puzo mythologizes. In another sense, they complement each other—Puzo glamorizing and Talese telling us not to worry. Perhaps the whole moral issue only exists in the heads of the noncriminally minded anyway. Non-Italian gangsters flourish very well without a myth. The black and Puerto Rican street gangs of New York, pushing for the latest in new legitimacies, may pick up some style hints from it. But the urge to set up private governments, police, and courts will presumably continue on its own steam until we achieve a common legitimacy, a Mafia of the people, as Bill Bonanno might say if he ever used the word, or split definitively into our constituent fragments.

As to the specific future of organized crime, *The Godfather* will no doubt do its little bit to sustain the slanderous impression that Italians have a lock on it. This is bad for the Mafia but good for everybody else in that line of work. Nicholas Gage, in his slapdash but readable book—sort of a Ripley approach to the subject—reports on a group of Italian carpenters who were held on suspicion for hours at the Heathrow Airport while Meyer Lansky slipped into England unnoticed to set up a huge gambling operation.

If the Mafia has an international future—if, that is,

it is to impose its hierarchic technique and legitimacy over the new electrosphere or global village—its high visibility will be a problem. But it has had this problem before in the United States and has solved it in every major city, regardless of Italian population. The Mafia knows how to work with outsiders as the British worked with the Fuzzy-Wuzzies, without losing identity. And it knows that a few Sicilians, maybe the fewer the better, go a long way. (The usual number cited is around 5,000 mafiosi in the U.S.)

Is the Mafia (outside of its undoubted entertainment value) worth the fuss? Again, like God, if it exists, it would seem to be pretty important. All that totally unaccountable money and power has to have political consequences. And the Mafia becomes more unaccountable by the minute, as operations tangle and ramify. President Nixon puts the gambling take at between 20 and 50 billion dollars a year, which by me is no information at all. If you can't get closer than that, you're just using your figures, like Luciano's corpses, for effect. Gage gives the Mob no more than 40 percent of the U.S. drug trade, which is still a nice piece of business if he's got it straight. But overall income is so diversified by now that it is harder to trace than the CIA use of foundation conduits. In fact, the same method is used—fungibility as it was called in the *Encounter* case: the laundering, or downright transubstantiation, of money by frequent reinvestment at home and abroad.

So it is possible (this much of the myth seems to be true) to work for the Mafia without realizing it. Their boast that they can get a man into the White House "and he won't know it till he gets the bill" may be just a flash of the old grandiloquence; at least its blundering attempts to get at the Kennedys through Sinatra (amusingly reported by Gage) suggest an idea whose time hadn't come. But a trail of corrupt officials, stultifying monopolies, and decayed cities is not bad to be going on with, for an organism within an organism, or cancer.

To conclude: a last word from the skeptics, and perhaps a Low-church compromise. If the Mafia does not exist, it would be baneful to believe in it. It gives us a Loch Ness monster to blame for all manner of local ills that need separate attention. It gives all of us the luxury of helplessness, and it gives politicians in particular an Orwellian cause, now that communism has slipped a bit, to raise funds for. (Curiously, the one with the richest opportunity, J. Edgar Hoover, denied the existence of the Mafia for years.)

A compromise would start with the lowest consensus: that there is such a thing as Big Crime, that it is more broadly organized than it used to be, and that Sicilian "families" play some part in it. The Death of the Mafia school maintains that the latter will soon be phased out, or will go relatively straight, and that crime, like prizefighting, will be taken over by the ambitious poor. It would be nice to think of the poor taking over such a large industry. But I think the argument overlooks just that largeness: the apparatus is there now like General Motors. A crook can't start out as he once could in a small way of business and hope to compete. You need capitalization and contacts and experience, and these the Mafia can provide pre-eminently, whether to Puerto Ricans working the numbers or Frenchmen refining heroin.

It could be that the Mafia will take an increasingly remote or entrepreneurial part in all this; and the Sicilian wing, or Mafia proper, is likely to see its name applied to more and more heathens until, like the Roman Church, it acknowledges Chinese *capos* and Nigerian *consiglieri*. But the Sicilian branch will probably retain a special place in the UN of crime, partly because it has the best myth and partly because it got there first, and established a grip on the machinery.

The new *capos* who can keep up with the wild bookkeeping will not be as much fun as the old ones—but then, as Stephen Potter would say, maybe they never were. The Golden Age is always just behind them. The new prototype is suggested by Bill Bonanno himself, suaver and better educated, and cooler in every way: like the latest Henry Ford compared with the old curmudgeon. The managerial revolution has, as usual, smoothed and dulled the reality. But the Mafia myth itself is in good shape, as suggested by the latest publishing lists and those lines at the movie. And if the myth was never true but always effective, why should not this continue to be so? *The Godfather* is like a recruiting poster for the Crusades. War isn't like that any more, and never was, but certain temperaments will follow the poster anyway. And, reinforced by these heavy injections from the media, the Mafia should be able to attract all the fiery young Corleones it needs, even if it's only to man the switch-

board and analyze the computer, and be snuffed out
at last by a missing credit card.

Wilfrid Sheed, well-known critic and novelist, graduated in history from Lincoln College, Oxford. A former editor of *Commonweal* magazine and movie critic for *Esquire*, he currently writes for such magazines as the *New York Review of Books*, the *New York Times Book Review*, and *Atlantic*. Three of his novels, *Office Politics*, *Max Jamison*, and *People Will Always Be Kind*, were nominated for the National Book Award.